To Paul...

All the Best
Luv Carrie Elwell

THE STREETS

Carrie Elwell

authorHOUSE®

AuthorHouse™ UK Ltd.
500 Avebury Boulevard
Central Milton Keynes, MK9 2BE
www.authorhouse.co.uk
Phone: 08001974150

First published by AuthorHouse 12/23/2009

ISBN: 978-1-4490-3782-6 (sc)

This book is printed on acid-free paper.

CONTENTS

CHAPTER ONE
DAY DREAMING

Sitting day dreaming by the pool on a lovely after noon sipping on my drink music blasting the sun is red hot sweat is running down my face .As I rub the sun cream in my body looking around the   massive garden and seeing the manor in its full glory .I feel so lucky I feel like my dreams have come true my prayers have been answered.

Thank GOD.

My name is Carrie I'm 31 yrs old I'm a very sophisticated young lady with class and a great sense of humor .Don't get me wrong I have had a long hard struggle to get where I am now .It is not as clear cut as it seems, my life has been filled with many dangerous downs.

I just found myself up the ladder and now I'm here I'm not climbing back down. It took a lot of blood sweat and tears pain hurt confusion abuse neglect to finally pull myself out of the vicious circle I was in.

Here I am today still alive to tell the story it sounds really scary when I say the words still alive, but its true I don't think anyone can begin to even imagine what I went through unless you are going through it yourself or have been. This book is for anyone who wants proof that there is light at the end of the tunnel. Maybe you are going through a rough time in your life and you need someone to reach out to, or you need that bit of hope and faith that there really is a brighter day .I would always pray for a better day I did get through the storms .Even though I said this book is for everyone I would like to think that it would help some people this is not a fiction book it's a fact that if you have will power and want to turn your life around you can ,all you have to do is try and you will succeed.

I did not one exam at school I would say I'm clever but in a different kind of way to brainy. I'm more clued up then any one and that's all down to the streets and the life I lead. I have night mares to this day I get a lot of flash backs .I feel like I'm always looking over my shoulder ,I still feel like I'm dreaming and that I'm not the person who I am now, what can I say apart from that's life.

Just had a long swim clear my head I've got a dinner party to attend tonight think I will need a bottle of vodka to .It's our neighbors Mr. and Mrs. Mills. They live near the village a ten minute drive from us .Lovely people nice house don't like eating out I'm very fussy and they are very posh not on my level at all. I'm more of a down to earth person definitely wasn't born with a silver spoon in my mouth. I would not be the person I am today if I had of been. Mr. and Mrs. Mills know this to ,but the only way to get to know who really stays at sea view manor is to socialize with us and invite us to any party they are having.

I'm friendly and sociable so I do go. Even if it's just for a laugh, I do like attention and I have always been told I have the gift of the gab I walk in to a room full of people and the whole room lights up. Looking back to when I was young hearing those words I didn't understand what it meant ,I thought it was just a figure of speech .Going to have some lunch with my darling baby boy Tyrone xx. My son is the best thing that's ever happened to me in my life and I love him more than anything in the world. He's 12 yrs old and the best son a mom could ever ask for. "Hi Ty, I finished my swim lets have some lunch it's your favorite pizza,"ok mom let me just finish this round on the game ".Putting the pizza in the oven to cook I stuck a piece of salmon in, I don't really like pizza. A message comes through on my phone,"hi I will come to the party with you l8ter hope Ty is ok, c u at about 6", we will have sum joke, x. It's my best mate sherry. We always have a laugh no matter where we go she is a class lady like myself .The only person I would talk to about anything personal because she understands me .She is just like me a great person Bless her .But really I keep friends at a far distance I don't like talking my business to anyone .Thinking of how friends had treated me in the past I get a cold chill run down my spine. I am young but have had a lot of experiences with so called friends and I think it is because my friends have not been there for me when I really needed them why I am the way I am today. "come on Ty lets go in to town for some bits and pieces .Driving through the village me and my son ,music pumping I think to myself how proud I am of my son ,who is such a inspiration and has give me so much strength and determination to carry on when I have been at my lowest Bless him I only had to look at his little cute face and he would give me so much hope and courage to carry on .It's always really only been me and my son ,his dad has never been around and no matter what man comes around me in our life ,he has never had that some one to call dad . I t hurts but there is nothing I can do. If I had of stayed with his dad God knows where I would be now .So I look at that as a positive thing and am so glad I'm away from all the madness .I m very independent and no I have not got a live in boy friend I have not got a husband I was married to Ty's dad got divorced by the age of 21 .I do have casual boyfriends umm and that's the way I like it.

Thinking of the first time I kissed a boy oh no how embracing , at infant school me and a mate both had boyfriends and we said at break time we will both kiss them , I'm laughing my head of writing this because I can see what happened in my head. Any way we all went in to the girls toilets them 2 in 1 toilet and us 2 in the other, we sat on the floor holding hands behind the door. As quite as anything so no one could hear when I finally got the courage to kiss him I did .Before I knew it I heard "what on earth do you think you are doing "the loudest and nastiest teacher Mr. Lawton ,what I couldn't believe it first kiss I can't even enjoy it .He rushed us out the toilet and then after break when all the class was in , he stood us all in front of the class and told the kids what we had been doing in the toilets , I was so upset It was all spoilt by that fat bald teacher I hated him . Funny now though memories….If I could go back and do it all again I wouldn't change a thing. My mom told me I was such a good girl when I was young .She always worried about me said I looked like a boxer when I was first born ,because the nurses dropped me on the floor the minute I was born and I was bruised.

Well that explains why I have always been a fighter. Going through primary school I had 2 good mates and they were boys. I was good I had lovely long brown hair. Cheeky smile I never got in trouble Mrs. Walker adored me .I had a thumb sucking problem and she was the only teacher who would let me stuck my thumb. Then one day a letter came home to say nits are going round the school, I give it to my mom. Then that evening I remember my dad saying he is going to cut my hair ,so I went to the kitchen he didn't even let me sit down all of a sudden I remember my hair dropping to the floor all of it , "I'm sick of your hair you sure are not going to be getting nits now". Tears rolled down my face I was in shock I never said a word my dad was to strict and I never said anything to him apart from hello and good bye. I wouldn't even sit in the same room and watch TV with him .I don't know why he has never done anything bad to me I was just scared of him. My hair was grade 2 short I looked in the mirror; I look like a boy I cried myself to sleep woke up the next morning a total different girl. We never had much money I always seen my mom finding it hard to survive no money she always tried her best for us , I love her so much she is really great with a heart of gold the best. From this day on I was a changed girl, this is how I knew I had switched. I was told by a teacher Mrs. mason to get a new book out of the store room, went in their first thing I saw was her handbag, I thought of how much my mom needed some money .I didn't even look in the purse I shoved it down my knickers and when we went to break I slipped it in my school bag. I couldn't wait to get home, just hope they don't notice while I'm here. Was the first out of school run all the way home? "Hi mom "I found this purse on the way home "she took it opened it counted out 70 pound in notes and some change."Do you no who's it is "no mom just keep it we need it "she burnt the purse in the back garden and we went to town. Having 70 pound in those days, especially when you got nothing is a lot, we had new clothes food my mom was happy, my brothers was happy I was happy that was a great day. I had to face the music the next day, it was on top next morning, police was called in questioning everyone I ran home and told my mom,"so it was the teachers purse you took then "yes don't send me back to that school again please "but you lied" I know but I didn't think .That was that I changed primary schools had a few weeks off then I went to the school over the main road.

With my short hair and no mates .I was nine seemed like no one liked me there was this one girl ,who thought she was the best all the girls was scared of her I wanted to be her friend. She was a proper bitch, took about 2 weeks to get to be mates with her, but she was horrible to me bossing me around showing off in front of the boys. After a bit I got fed up of her I hated her the way she talked to me calling me names. I wanted to get her back she is all mouth. One break time she was giving it the big one in the play ground and I flipped I kicked the shit out of her, in front of everyone teachers to. She was finished from that day it was me who runs this school. I got sent home had to stay off school for a week. My mom didn't say much , weekend I was out playing ,never forget me and 3 mates these lads who I always hang around with they was like brothers. We said we are going to rob sum plants to sell to make some money. A few streets away from where I lived we were robbing. I picked up one plant pot from by the front door to my surprise I found the key I called the others "look what I got "what you going to do with it "in a scared manor they asked."What do you think "no don't "don't Carrie you will get in trouble" shut up" I said opened the door in the bedroom got a bag filled it with worthless jewelry and off home I went. Well them lot just stood there when I was robbing the stuff , one of the lads went home and must of told his mom, remember I m still only 9 yrs old. .then bang the door shit its pc Branford the local bobby. "Carrie get here now "that was it I was in big trouble "I can be sure of it that as soon as you are 12 old enough to be arrested ,I will be here to lock you up", quite I said a word I give the bag of stuff back. I had the biggest beating ever my mom beat me with my roller skate there was a hole in my bedroom wall where I had ducked out the way. I didn't cry was angry I knew who grassed me up.

Party time "let's go and show our face then at the mills. Me Ty and sherry walk in the house smiling saying hello. They just all look at my legs and breast first any way even the women in shock of how sexy I am. Funny to see the way people react to me, I love it you either love me or hate me. I just play people up even more if I think you are on a bad vibe I can't help it. Thinking back to how I was when I was young I was worse because if I thought someone didn't like me I would beat them up no matter how big. I start feeling a bit guilty because I have done some nasty things ,like when I was 11 this boy up the road from us he was 16 , really got on my nerves yet when I think about it he never said a word to me I just hated him, for no reason . I caught him one day walking past the park I had some white heeled shoes on and he got battered with them I just lashed out at him , smacked him over the head with the shoes and he run home crying.. why did I do that I really hurt him .any way his mom came down our house moaning to my mom showing her what I had done, my mom just said fuck off our Carrie is only 11 he is 16 get a life. that was that but having so much anger in me to lash out for no reason kind of scared me .I am not going to be lashing out here or any where again ,I have learnt to control my anger where ever it comes from. As I'm day dreaming cutting out the voices in the room I suddenly hear "Carrie how are you I have been trying to call you "I can do without the chat up lines now and if he has got no response when he calls that spells it out. "Alright I've been really busy, had no time "I had to cut this short because I don't like over staying my welcome in other words I was ready to get the fuck out of there. I got Tyrone and sherry and said our goodbyes. "so it's a mad one tonight the driver is going to be here soon so we can get hammered tonight in Manchester. I love Manchester even though I'm like one and a half hours drive from there I still go there on a regular .I used to live there in fact I ran away to Manchester to get away from my sons crazy dad, or at least I tried to. He was not a nice man at all and no matter how hard I would try I could never get away from him, Going back to the time when I found out I was pregnant .we was living or should I say hiding out at his sister's house .she had used to be my best friend but you will hear about her later .Any way he was on crack bad and we had nothing everything we was getting was going on crack. I hated living like this and I was scared because I was trapped .I Must have been really ill one day the Dr came out and all I remember is when he felt my belly and then shoved his hand up my fanny and said, oh you are so pregnant .confused I just thought straight away no matter what happens I'm having this baby and I got to be careful. That idiot was upstairs getting paranoid because the Dr was there. I was happy he didn't really say anything when I told him ,just licked another shoot on the crack pipe .Time went on and he treated me so bad all through my pregnancy I used to shop lift to get money and I stole lots of little boys baby clothes and had keep my babies things in bags so I had clothes for my baby .one night he had smoked all the crack and said "I going to prawn the baby clothes, get them out" by this time I hated him I was just so scared I couldn't say no incase he hit me and hurt the baby. I got the clothes tears rolled down my face because I knew we wasn't getting them back and that was all I had for my baby .He took the clothes to a lady who bought stuff off us, she give him the money for the clothes then the next day she gave them back to me, bless her I didn't know I was having a boy I just guessed and was drawn to nicking boys clothes. Bearing in mind I meet this man when I was 15 and had been trapped ever since. By this time the council had give us a flat and I tried to make it feel homely but then he always messed everything up for me. One day he had took some shit 'crack 'but he called it shit off these dealers outside the flat .he run through the back door and left them out the front . I watched from the window then a few minutes later the door is getting smashed down I was carping myself, but I stood behind the door they ran in shouting where the fuck is he .two guys they had a garden fork in their hand, they looked around and came up to me I said I don't know, they just looked at me and looked at my belly and left. When they had gone I sat with my head in my hands and cried I'm just a little girl I don't know where this is going to end, I had nothing in the flat much so they couldn't take anything for payment because there was nothing. they could of hurt me because of that bastard ,yes that's what he is a bastard and I hated him I will get him back .I knew when to get my revenge ,when he was off his head ,now this man was 17 years older than me but I knew when I could kick fuck out of him , you see all these things that keep on building up day after day the time will come when I will go mental on him .All the shit that he had done to me and that he kept doing to me was eating me up inside .

Remember I have always had a short temper ever since I was little. He always said oh I'm sorry babes and I just ignored him .every morning we would wake up the first thing he would say to me is where we going shopping today .I wanted to be someone else I didn't want to be in this situation no more my baby will be here soon I got to get a proper life. But this is all I had no one could save me not my mom dad police any one I'm stuck with this shit head. I was getting depressed. I had a lot of charges on my head I had been on probation since I was 13 social workers had always been part of my life. If I got caught shoplifting again that was it prison. Going along with his plans I did get caught again this time I got remanded to custody .I didn't care at least me and my baby was safe .was in jail for two weeks and on sentencing the judge let me off lightly because my baby was due .So I'm out straight away he was on me we got a house in the ghetto as we had lost the flat when I went jail and it got trashed by the police who was looking for that cunt .The house was nice I did my best I had no idea how I was going to cope when my baby was born I don't even know how to prepare the baby food .he was still being horrible smoking shit having every tom dick and harry in when I was asleep. Sometimes I would wake up and go down stairs the front door would be wide open .I was scared because he's mad and I no he is I'm still a kid but I know what I have seen so far and that is not right .I just kept quiet and out of the way .one day I went to the shop on the way home finally my water had broke .but I was getting no pain. I didn't know what to expect so got to hospital and they said they would have to give me some stuff to start the labor .I was in pain high as a kite off the gas, all I remember is the midwife bless her saying what a long piece of leg him have .she was a lovely women may she rest in peace who knew the family my little brother used to hang around with her grandson. That was it my boy is here he is lovely had thick black hair on his ears and was red and swooshed up ,I loved him the second I set eyes on him he's so cute .I had to go to surgery when he was born as the after birth never came out .

I was so ill my whole body felt in agony .The baby grow didn't fit him his legs was to long he is the best. Then in walks that idiot with a mate cracked off their heads, "get dressed we are going to get some stuff from this shop I got this man to drive us", I was ill and was not going anywhere so there was a big argument and the staffs throw them out. I cried how he could, he has not even held the baby and he wants me to go shop lifting and I can't even walk. He should be bringing me flowers and saying thank you. My mom was with me and was upset to but she was also scared of this freak that's why I could never get saved no one would get involved they just left me to it. You made your bed you lie in it, that's all I was told when I tried to talk about P. what I was going to do was I going to end up going insane with this freak.

My mom used to say you could kill him and they would let you off all the stuff he has done to you. I was beginning to think that was all I could do to get away from him , They discharged me from hospital I got in a taxi with my baby Tyrone I had a name for my boy . I was worried on the way home I knew what had been going on and I knew the police was after him and a lot of dealers ,pulled up in the cab ,there was no front door just a board up I couldn't get in had to go round the back .the police had smashed yet another door in looking for him .I was depressed but I carried on I was too concerned with how to look after my baby , I didn't even know how to make a bottle no one had not give me any advice what so ever , he would be in and out and doing my head in , so bad one day I couldn't take his mental pressure I grabbed the knife out the draw and wanted to stab him I wanted to kill him. Then I just couldn't do it I didn't have the balls I was not about to spend ten years in jail for this fool .So I stabbed myself instead in my leg it was bleeding bad so I got my baby and I went to my mom's they took me to hospital to make sure I hadn't cut a vessel and that was that. I said to my mom I'm not going back there. I knew some girls from Manchester who I had been in prison with a few years ago when I got bird for kidnapping and robbery at the age of 15.but you will hear about that later on. I called them up, they said come down we will sort you out with a place to live. That was just what I wanted to hear just as I'm getting a few clothes from the house who turns up .that bastard I was going and told him that I had a lift and was ready me and Tyrone got in the car and he got in the car to "I'm coming with you". So I went along with it just so there was no trouble .thinking along the way trapped again I hate this man so much. I mean if you check it out I have never done anything to this man and I did not deserve to be treated the way he had been treating me from the day I meet him. If in this day and age any man abuses a young 15 year old girl not just physically, mentally to. Well what can I say apart from he would be classed as a pedophile in my book and if my 15 year old daughter had been in his hands then I would have killed him myself. I'm not saying that I was innocent because I was a corrupt young girl but please I went through hell and back with him I don't know how I survived. But if it's one lesson I have been taught in life and that's how to be a fighter no matter what situation you are facing. I had to be strong I kept my faith in God and prayed please protect me and my son. I knew anything could happen with a mad man like him.

CHAPTER TWO
PARTY TIME

Me and sherry had vodka and red bull in the back of the range on the motor way this guy who is driving is a really good driver I didn't drive with just anyone .we was laughing and joking pulled up outside the club got out heard the music and went on a mad one .Now I have been raving since the age of 13 in night clubs dark underground parties blues. Those were the days I had so much fun .I went to a hit man and her show that was at our club in town it was always on t v and I was there, every one seen it on t v I was on the stage talking to a presenter for the show me and two other girls had to beat 3 men in a competition who can get the key through the clothes quicker wins. Well of course we had nothing on hardly so we won a video with some chill out music on. Then their used to be a rave every Saturday night in the town top M C's and D J's I would be buzzing I took trips a lot acid and would be on a buzz every day of the week me and my two best mates they were sisters the roughest girls ever, don't cross them they will fuck you up big time. But the 3 of us were like 3 peas in a pod always together up to no good .they are what I call proper hardcore girls. We would go to the holiday inn heated car park after this club loads of us from the club and blast tunes smoke weed dance it was like a party .then the warehouse raves where everyone is so high and buzzed up the vibes was so good ,it will never be like back in the day .I sniffed poppers and one time when I had ecstasy and acid I went blind for 5 minutes I was a mess on these drugs I drank lots of drink smoke weed had crack I was proper un aware what I could of done to myself. I mean some parties people would say open your mouth and that was that another E. I don't do drugs now at all only smoke weed. Will I ever give up, not just yet that's the only drug that can calm me down and chill me out.

I do get a lot of flash backs of the drugs I used to take and all the things I have been through   I'm to hyper .I don't drink a lot but once a week will have a good one. I have been in clubs where people have got shot and trouble has kicked off .I remember one night when I had taken so many drugs I was out of my head didn't know what I was doing at all. Then there is the down side to clubbing which really put me off everything and luckily enough I'm still here to explain what happened. It's something I have put behind me now ,as hard as it was to get my head around what had happened .I was dancing at this local bar where they played house and garage music , just minding my own business having a good time .all of a sudden smack ,this bitch had smacked me around the jaw with a bottle. In shock I automatically beat the shit out of her. After that I went to the toilets to check out my face , it was fine not one cut .Sweet I just carried on enjoying myself .The club had finished and we was walking along the road when my friend said ,run Carrie he has a knife. I didn't think twice because I had got stabbed when

I was 15 already and that was bad ,I just ran he caught up with me all I remember is him grabbing my hair and stabbing me in my head ,he kept stabbing me ,I had to fight him off and by this time that bitch who started the trouble in the first place was on me to ,so I had to fight the two of them together otherwise they would of killed me. There was a crowd standing round, people who knew me, my so called best mates. They stood there and watched me get stabbed up .lucky for me I had a bag around my chest with phone and keys ,that was slashed up .just think if I never had that bag on I would have been killed. After a bit they broke away cause I had to fight for my life .I remember having that bitch on the floor and the man running round me slashing my arms up. If I had of stood there I would have been finished off. Got myself together walked off blood pouring from my head my arms were red it had got sliced bad over my arm and I could see inside my arm .My so called mates got in a taxi with me and went to hospital. All I was worried about was my hair it was red thick with blood ,and my little boy he's only 3why is this happening to me why .I was strong got stitched up and went home to my baby .I couldn't do anything my arms were bandaged from top to bottom ,I lay in my bed and cried I felt hopeless I couldn't even hold my son that was the hardest part I couldn't even pick my baby up and hug him I was finished I felt like it was the end of the world. That shit what happened that night fucked my head up it was in the papers the two bastards who done it got locked up ,they was at the hospital the same time as me, I must of hurt that bitch I had to I had to fight for my life ,Looking at the bag I had on at the time that saved my life it had slash marks on it, if I didn't have it on I would have been stabbed in my heart, I knew for a fact that I had a guardian angel , I thanked God I was alive and tried to heel and be strong for my little boy.

Ty's dad was in prison at this time I was still on and off with him at this stage because I was still married to he and I went to see him every week in jail. So of course this had made me very scared being alone with no one to help us ,This is bringing back so many bad memories because if I hadn't of got cut up I wouldn't of meet this man .I had a doctor's appointment one day to see how my arms was heeling ,doing ok I walked back home just before I got to the bottom of the street I heard a voice "whapped baby ".I looked round and saw a tall dark thin man ,"What's going on with your arms" ,he was a yardie I could tell I hadn't seen him around before I was feeling scared and insecure and needed someone to talk to I had no one . I said "this man stabbed me ".he said "where you live I will come round and have a chat with you and get him sorted out. Those words were the words I had been waiting to hear, like a twat I told him where I live. Next thing you no he is at the door, letting him in he said he is well known no one is not fucking with me now. He came round at least two times before he wanted to have sex, I said yes but not without protection. He never clicked with my son and I didn't like him I just couldn't say no to him ,he was persistent I was scared because he never mentioned the situation with my arms I felt he had ultimate motives . He would say you are going on holiday to Jamaica, I didn't want to I knew why he wanted me to go .He gave me some crack to sell because I lived in an area where there was a lot of drug abuse. He gave me about 300 pounds worth and had wrapped it out and said start it up and get some money. I did because I needed cash to get out of this being penniless shit. One of my best mates was in on me then she always abused drugs from as long as I can remember, I did ok the first few times I got rid of it all he gave me money and that .then one night I smoked a spiff of crack and smoked another and I smoked the lot me and my mate. I was wired and hadn't thought about paying the money back. Any way she went and when he came round for the money I didn't have it. He was angry he said my son is evil and he pulled me upstairs to the bed where my son was sleeping and forced himself on me .I kept saying no, no get a condom, he told me to shut the fuck up or else he'll kill me and my boy .I was scared I just let him carry on he got up and left. I never seen him again .I felt like I had been raped ,I felt dirty my poor boy had to see that bastard on top of me fucking me , when I don't want him on me . I was messed up now big time.

I had made friends with people through selling the drugs .there was one guy who robbed pubs and cars he was on crack and had feel out with his baby mother. He said if I let him stay he will look after me with money and that because he was a raiser. I said ok I needed someone just to be around us after what had gone on with that yardie. He was strange and would lock himself in the bathroom and wouldn't come out for hours, I had enough so one day I kicked the door in and saw him shooting up his veins with a needle. .I ran downstairs when he come down I said you got to go I got my baby here you can't do that. He didn't like it he grabbed the hammer that he used to rob these pubs and said he is going to fucking smash my head in if I don't give him my gold chain. Well this chain in question had a clown on the end of it and it had strange powers. Like I was on the road one day and I was talking to a nice guy who I got on with and all of a sudden the chain dropped of my neck on to the floor .Thinking nothing of it I picked it up and carried on .But the poor guy got shot in his flat and died, don't know who done it why or anything .May he rest in peace Mario, I thought to myself the chain had tried to tell me something when I found out he had been murdered. I didn't want to give him the chain it was mine, but my life is worth more than gold. I give it him and he went. I just couldn't believe it how can one bad situation lead to another then

to another. Where's it going to end .I had to get out that
house it wasn't good for me. Trying to be strong I enrolled at
college and got to study while my son was in the play group
at college. One afternoon I came home my house had been
robbed .That was it I moving out, I got a house out of the
area and tried again. I made mates and got a job on the side,
in a ware house and was saving to take my baby to Ibiza.
I had always wanted to travel and now I had 2 get my act
together and sort our life out. I had no one at all to guide
me through life, ever since I'd been 13, I was doing whatever
I wanted to and no one or nothing could stop me .so I need
to grow up and stop this fucked up way of living and make
a good life for me and my sweet baby boy .ever since the
day I was pregnant I knew that no matter what my child
would come first before any one and anything. When I look
back on how things was for me and how many times I felt
my life was in someone else's hands, if only these bastards
that held the weapons in their hands realized the pain and
grief it brings to people, then maybe they would think about
what they are doing before they do it. I can truly say I'm one
of the lucky ones so many people have had their lives taken
from them for no reason. I feel so grateful for life and what I
have got and I now understand that there is a better way no
matter what situation you are in ,Even through the darkest
lowest points in my life I always kept my faith in God . I no
sometimes things just seem so hard and you may feel like
you are trapped in a situation and there's no way out .but
everyone is born free and no one needs to suffer at the hands
of another person or the life style you live, there has always
got to be a plan b. Plan b to me is to believe in yourself
and your mind will guide you, always be head strong as will
power will get you a long way. From my experiences with
such a dangerous life style at such a young age I would say to
get as far away as possible from any uncertain situations you
are in, if there is no escape then plan one. There has always

got to be a way out. I see that now I didn't before I just felt like this is it, this is how it's always going to be.

Now I'm away from the danger I'm so happy and I'm sure that's all anyone wants is to be happy. I never thought I would make it I had no education and was totally lost out there in the big bad world. I found myself now and all my knowledge is self taught , I don't have no degrees but I think I have done pretty well for myself and only have myself to thank for it ,so do yourself a favor and whatever goal you set in life aim to score . Life is only what you make it I could of gone crazy a long time ago because at one time in my life I thought I was going to crack up. But I held my mind together and cracked the code of life don't let nothing or no one drag you down , some people are to jealous and hate to see you progress most of these people are your mates or so called. Best to leave the haters alone I can read people good and can tell when someone is a genuine friend or not . People don't know how to take me some times but I m a straight to the point sort of person, it's the best way to be I don't hold my mouth or thoughts for no one if I want to say something I will. If you want to be heard in life it's the only way I have a lot of confidence in myself and that alone has got me along way. It took me some years to realize that I had these key skills to help me through life but when I did I used them to my advantage. don't let nothing block the road for me again because I'm coming through .once I had picked up on things in my mind I knew that I was finally ready to change my life and I was determined to succeed.

CHAPTER THREE
FROM THE START

I am not going to mess about no more I'm going to tell you how my life has been .I m through with confusion and distraction .so I'm going to be straight from the start . I love my family with all my heart and do not hold any one responsible for what happened to me in my life what so ever .like I said I love my mom with all my heart and would never want to upset her in any way . She has always tried to be there for me and I respect her so much she is the loveliest woman ever. But knowing what I know now how much worry and stress I caused her it's unbelievable and I m truly sorry. I just didn't understand and didn't care about any ones feelings. Now I am a mother I totally understand that once you have a child they become your whole life and I know I caused my mom a lot of trouble ,and once again I can't express the fact that I'm truly sorry. We are very close now and always there for each other.

From the day my dad cut my hair off that was it I was a tom boy .drinking smoking steeling fighting it's like something switched in my head and there I was bad Carrie. I had been expelled from primary school and was due to start secondary school, I got kicked out through fighting with the girl who I hated more than anyone in the school. She was a bully until I bet her up ,it's like she would manipulate people and make them look small, every time I seen her she got battered. Got to high school on the first day I bet the same girl up again really bad and got expelled on my first day .I didn't care I wanted to take my anger out on someone ,she was the one who got me kicked out of primary and she is going to know about it . Any way she moved school by the time I went back and everyone in the school had heard about me beating this girl up on my first day. I had a reputation from day one the teachers all hated me. I was not at all interested in school I enjoyed English history and PE. But I got in with the big boys at school and was in the gang who run everything in the school. I was in love with a boy James and we would be together all the time with this gang of lads. I was the only girl permitted because of James. By this time my hair had grown a bit and I had a perm on top still short at the back.

I am pretty but have a bad character and that is what drawn people to me from an early age. I have always wanted to be the centre of attention and that is exactly what I was. I would not spend much time at home and would always be up to no good. I did not learn much at school was always in trouble. Then it got to a point where I was walking in class for a mark in register and walking back out down to the shops to meet up with my boyfriend and his mates. They always had lots of drugs money and things on them, they all went to my school but was a bit older than me. They were sweet we would smoke weed and drink over the fields all day and night, and then I would sometimes sleep at my boyfriend's house when his Nan and Granddad was at work. I would not tell my mom would just face the music in the morning .we had sex and I loved him so much it went on like this through the year I was 13 . I was not allowed on a trip to France to go. I was told when they got back that this girl had been going out with James in France. I lost it he broke my heart and I got myself kicked out of school for good for beating the crap out of this girl. Well I lost my temper so easy she got a lot more than even I expected.

That night James had told his friends to meet me by the shops and tell me that he had finished with me for good. I was heartbroken .I cried and cried and cried the lads were there to comfort me. "We will cheer you up "they said these guys were 15 there was 3 off them that night so we got loads of drinks from the shop and went over the fields. I had so much drink and drugs I was off my face I didn't know what I was doing. They had give me a tablet to try and all I remember is a women finding me by the pub down the road from my mom's house. She took me home as she knew me and my mom. I kept just thinking what has happened to me ,what has happened ,my mom was angry throw me in a cold bath of water and smacked me right up my face about ten times .really hard to bring me round and then put me in bed. I just didn't know what had happened what had they done to me because I don't remember a thing and it couldn't be the drink alone, I was so confused but couldn't do anything about it I had a bad feeling but didn't know what they had done to me and how did I end up at the pub I can't remember a thing. It scared me a lot.

A few days after I went to my mates she lived in the ghetto so to speak and I got mixed up with some girls. Two sisters they were safe smoked weed and went shoplifting made quite a bit of money from it to. So I started hanging around with them we were as thick as thieves and I was easily led so I would go with whatever was going on. We would rave hard take E's and acid I moved out of my mom's house and was living with these two sisters they were older than me .I liked the excitement ,we would go shoplifting everyday and then go out raving . We always put money together for hired cars to go on missions and get where ever we wanted. I got locked up a lot for the same old thing time and time again shoplifting. I was good at it and would make at least 200 pound a day some times ,then there was times where we would get locked up .my mom had to bail me out every time and after about 90 convictions the judge remand me to care of the local authority . I had to go to a kids home I was 14 at this stage in my life and didn't know what I was doing and didn't think about the fact that I'm 14 got kicked out of school at 13 no exams no sexual education my mom never talked to me about anything like that I was never in that's why and now I had been put in a gritty kids home with no money no drugs no drink no raving, what was I going to do,

I got hold of a can of gas of some other kids that was in there and sniffed it. My head felt like it was going to explode I was so ill I couldn't tell the staff my head was pounding I had half the can and I felt like I was going to die serious I really did it was that bad and as I'm writing this now one of the headaches has come on what I have had ever since I sniffed that gas can that one time, it's bad and I never ever did it again after that it scared me. I got myself together and started going back to fire town where my mates lived .I was uncontrollable and did what I wanted to do no matter what .My mates were ok but after a bit I started to not like one of the sisters and was closer to the other one .she would steal money and things from me I didn't like it she was shady and the other sister was nice we had a connection. I was still getting in to more and more trouble and I had a lot of charges hanging over my head I was on supervision order since 13 and had to see social workers a lot. I did a runner from the home went back to my mates .they had a older brother who was due to come out of prison soon his name was p I went with one of the sisters one day to a prison visit he was charming and that . Then he started writing to me and sending me nice pomes I was overwhelmed I liked it. I felt special for once .But as it goes I was in court and didn't turn up when the police finally caught up with me they locked me up. I was 15 and got 3 months in jail for all the charges I had committed. I wasn't bothered they sent me to a women's prison in liver pool I didn't know what to expect but because there was no young offenders jail's for girls I had to go to this prison. When I got their I was a bit scared got in reception and was some Liverpool girls and some Manchester girls and it seemed alright got checked In and had some tea was waiting to be taken to the wing . I don't really think the women released I was only 15 because I was so grown up. Well I went to the hospital wing as I was too young to go on the wing you had to be 16 or over. Oh it was horrible was surrounded by these idiots who lived for the medication and was not on my level at all. I hated it the next day the screws got me doing jobs like cleaning the toilet. I said I am not doing it and this one big bitch screw said I have got to. I said no you fucking do it. She jumped on me with another screw and dragged me to a cell padded with nothing in. I sat there and thought well this is better than being in a room full of freaks because that's all there was on a hospital wing in prison. Women that are hiding from the others on the wing I didn't want to be there. On hearing the governor looked at my file and said you are only 15 you shouldn't be here really we got to get you a transfer. Any way by the Monday I was on my way to an open prison and there was a better chance for me to do my time instead of being stuck on a hospital wing. I got to the new jail I liked it, made friends girls had weed it was proper class. I will never forget was around Christmas time and they was making homemade hooch so we could all get pissed. I had kicked off a few times and with the screws and they sent me to anger management lesions. I didn't take know notice of what they were talking about and just did what I had to do to stay out the block. I easily fitted in with the main girls in the jail and was never an outcast was in on everything. I didn't for one minute regret being in prison in fact I felt safe for once in my life and enjoyed it. My time went quick only ended up doing two months ,when I came out I went straight back to fire town the only place I knew ,as I didn't want to go back to my mom's I had changed been in prison and knew I had to look after myself and survive on my own.

My family had enough of me and I did feel like an outcast as I was to hyperactive and could not face sitting in my bedroom and being bored. I had no mates around my parents area and nothing to go back for .The day I got released I remember standing at the train station with another girl who got let out the same day as me .she was ok but proper hooked on drugs, all she kept saying was hurry up I got to get a fix .I just thought how can someone be let out of jail and all she wants is drugs. At this point in my life I was not addicted to hard drugs and knew I was head strong cause I just done a bird and was only 15. Was wishing all the way back that my life was different and I didn't want to keep getting in trouble with the police. I had no one to turn to so I had no choice things just had to go the way they did .and even if I ended up sleeping in the street hopefully there would be a way out. I got to my mates they knew I was coming because we all wrote to each other when I was locked up. I knew as soon as I walked in that there was a change in vibe."My brothers out of jail and he's staying here". I didn't know anything about this man apart from he had been in prison for a long time. I was a little girl really at heart and was innocent no matter what I had been through so far, with the fact that I may have been raped that time when I was left by the pub and had never spoke to anyone about it and the fact that I had so much anger inside me that it scared me because I didn't know where it was coming from. I was still a young girl who was not told anything about anything and had to learn the hard way. I never seemed to have any luck. I would act as if I was ok but deep down I knew I wasn't.

I knew that everyone was on edge because P was out but I didn't say anything. Then a bang at the door it was him "yes my baby love you are out" he came up to me and give me a hug. He had a woman with him. The sisters was acting dodgy .he went upstairs one of the sisters started moaning "fucking cunt he better not be bringing these dirty bitches here .she was angry then she went up stairs and started kicking off with him. He gave her a stone and she went off to build a joint. Oh well I went to the front line and thought I'd buy a rock and smoke it. I told my mates I'm going in the bath and locked the door. Had a nice hot bath and smoked my rock in a joint I was buzzing. Bang the fucking bath room door came off P had kicked the bathroom door in and punched me in my head and said "you are taking to fucking long in here dragged me out the bath room, I wasn't even dressed. I was in shock he had no right to do that to me I was not his girl so why do that. I was confused and scared because I knew everyone was scared of him I could tell. My mates never said anything I just went back over the front and got another stone. I was talking to some guys for a bit and went back to my mates. P was in the flat he looked angry he said "give me the fucking stone I saw you over their talking to that bastard." I ran upstairs he chased me I was so scared I did not know this man, no one has been able to tell me anything all my life and he is just so scary I just want to run away and hide. He was on his own no women was with him and he came in the bed room looked at me then ripped the curtain pole down from the window and beat the living day light out of me with this pole . His sister was screaming stop P stop. He didn't he just carried on I was black and blue from head to toe my hands had massive lumps over them where I had tried to protect myself from the beatings. I was a mess I was scared and I had no one who could help me now. I knew there was no turning back no getting back on that train to jail where I was safe ,this is it trapped with no life my mind was brainwashed ,I couldn't think for myself P was evil he was possessed I was petrified .

I was in shock for days I did not move out that bedroom. Then he came in and started kissing me and playing with my body. I was never the sort of girl to run to the police because I had been in so much trouble and in the ghetto a police informer is the last thing I want to be called. I held it down and was too scared to tell him to stop. He said you are my girl now, my baby love. I did not like him at all but what could I have done. I had no one I knew nothing else and had to stay here because this is where I came back to. I was 15 going through all of this abuse on my own. My mates knew what he was like they warned me don't get involved with him he is bad news. It was too late I had no choice but to do what he said. He would take me shoplifting and take all the money off me for drugs ,he did give me a joint to smoke but as for food ,well no we never eat much and was together all the time he did not let me out of his sight. My mates were angry cause I was with him all the time, they'd say don't fuck about with him, but what could I do how can I get out of this situation. It soon got round that me and him were together, he was much older than me 34 when I meet him. People would say to me when we was on street together what are you doing with him. I would walk behind him like a lost little sheep. Could no one see that I was being abused by him, or were they to scared to say anything to him; he was always beating man up over drugs or robbing them. I was just lost in the streets and how would I get away from him. The sex was twice a day morning and night. He would just do what he wanted to me .I didn't know much about sex or men so I would just lay their cold as ice on my back, I didn't enjoy it he was a beast.

He let me call my mom from time to time I told her about him she said you made your bed you lie in it. She didn't understand how bad it was. I would cry when he was not in the room but I could not go anywhere without him with me. I was messed up big time I felt like a robot being told what to do and I had to do it or I knew how bad the beatings were. We went to my mom's one day and he meets my mom. "The famous P I have heard so much about you, how much of a gangster you are."He laughed and shook her hand and charmed her. I thought to myself gangster he is a fucking cunt and I hate him. I said hello and was off on the road .the car broke down on a dual carriage way. He told me to push the car so he could jump start it. So I did was pushing and it had started he was driving because we started to go down a hill I had held myself up off the road on the car. He was going fast I was holding on by my arms and knew if I let go I was finished , I held on for my life ,he came off the dual carriage way and stopped I was shouting you idiot I was on the back of the car. He laughed. I was upset I could of dropped off the car and been killed. He didn't care. This was the case I had learned to try and like him to make things easy for myself I knew I was stuck with him and that was that. He would talk to himself while we was having sex and talk about another man being in the room watching him fucking me ,I would just cringe and lie there. It got on top in fire town so he said we are going to London because he wants to get away from all the shit.

I knew he was a pimp and I was not sure of going to London it sounds so far away all I know is here. Went any way had no choice he did try to be ok with me sometimes only when he wanted me to do something for him. He said we are going to get a hotel and stay up here for a bit. After being with this beast I had really calmed down and gone really sad. I just did as he said I felt like a zombie. We got to Euston he got a hotel on kings cross. I knew he had a son and an ex misses in London but he never said he was going to be visiting them. He said I got a plan I want some money so you go and stand on the street and bring any man you can back to the hotel, I will be watching you and when you go in the room tell them to take their clothes off and I will bust in the room and deal with their pussy clart. "Go on then start walking" I just looked at him and went. I stood outside the train station; men were walking up to me saying how much. I was a 15 year old girl on the street about to rob people. I looked like a kid to, I had no dress sense and I had no nice clothes how can these sick wankers want to pay to have sex with me. I thought none of you are going to touch me. P had promised me that no one could touch me, I had to believe in him. It weren't long before I was walking back to the hotel with a punter. Got him in the room and told him to pay me 40 pound. And take his clothes off. He did then bang, went the door "what the blood clart you doing pussy boy, with my daughter she is only 15". The punter shit himself P emptied his wallet and punched him up, I just stood there. Was glad it worked out like that, I didn't have to do nothing with the men but just the thought of having to even speak to a strange man scared me they could be any mad man, one of them could have killed me. "Go on get another one", I did as he said and it went on and on like that. After robbing people and then going to stand in the same place I had picked these punters up from, didn't cross my mind that they could come back and look for me. Then a man walked up to me and smacked me right in my face and walked off. I was scared he must have been one we robbed that day, but there was so many I could not remember them. One thing is good that P kept his word and did not let anyone touch me. But he was nowhere to be seen when that man hit me. I was just glad that all he did was hit me, he could of done anything to me I wouldn't of been none of the wiser.

We had a bit of money I never had none he had it all. We got on top in that area so moved to north London but he had cracked out all the money and we needed a bath. He said I got a place where we can have a shower at my son's house. The mom was not in the son was but p told him to go in the bedroom .the son was only 12. I had a bath and was getting dressed, his ex walked in. She went mad at him, and said to me you will never get anywhere with him get out. He told me to wait in the car. So I did hour after hour all night he still didn't come down. I went to sleep in the car, the police woke me up, "what are you doing "shining the touch in my face. "I'm waiting for my friend "where do they live we need address. I had to tell them which flat he was in or else they was going to lock me up if they thought I was telling lies. I told them they went up and checked out the storey don't know what crap they told the police but it worked. Just as day light broke he was there in a bad mood "what the fuck you tell the police where I was for". Before I could answer smack in my face, grabbing me saying "we are going to make some fuck money to day you hear me bitch". I was hungry cold and scared. I just did what he said and was back on the streets robbing people.

We made a lot of money and he said he wants to go back to fire town to see his sisters. I wanted to see my mom I was glad he dropped me to see my mom for ten minutes, I was really happy to see her. He then went to his sisters and left me with them while he went over the pub on front line. They were being nasty with me and didn't want to talk to me, I left after a while walked over to the pub. A guy ran up to me with a knife in his hand and went to stab me in my face , I automatically put my hands up to stop the knife going in to my face . It went straight through my hand my left one and came out the other side. He stabbed me in my right hand to but it wasn't as bad as my left. I didn't feel the knife go in I ran in the pub and put my hand in the ice bucket. Blood was pouring fast from my hand I wrapped a shawl around my hand real tight to try to stop the bleeding. No one helped me, why had he done it I don't even know him; I went in to a state of shook then in came P and told me to go with him. I just followed him I thought I was going to get killed the fear rushed through my body as my hands poured out blood. I had to think fast he took me to a flat up in the 12 floor a crack heads house , I didn't cry I knew I had to save myself from bleeding to death ,he told me in the lift that I can't go to the hospital as they would think he had done it . I was so scared I held the shawl round my left hand tighter and tighter my whole body was shaking. We got in the flat he sat me down in the living room for a few minutes I sat there and watched them smoke the shit. They didn't pay me any mind was too concerned in the drugs. I told p I was going to the bath room I knew I had to be claim because that p would batter me if I wasn't. I got in bathroom and remember sitting on the side of the bath for what seemed like hours running my hand under the cold tap to thumb my hand .I felt terrible I cried to myself I just want to see my mom please God help me .After hours of what seemed like a blur I felt like I was going to pass out then I saw him standing in the door way, come on I'm going to let you go to the hospital now. At last didn't think I was going to get there ,at the hospital at 5 in the morning I was all alone he was waiting around outside they asked how it happened and I said a man had walked up to me and stabbed me through the hands .I didn't know him which is what happened but I knew his street name but that was it .They cleaned me up and stitched my right hand up ,told me I had to see a doctor at 9 am .I wanted to see my mom but knew I had to tell him what was happening so I told them I would be back at 9. Meet up with him I didn't say nothing I just wanted to see my mom I needed her to help me we knocked them up my dad just opened the door and let us in, I said I needed to see mom when she got up and I just lay there, he lay next to me hugging me, I hated him so much why was this happening to me all through him. I knew that tangos had stabbed me because he robbed some shit of him. Just because he couldn't do him nothing, the bastard took it out on me because he knew I was P's girl. It just seemed so unjust I didn't understand but one thing I did understand is that cunt went to stab me in my face and if I had not of put my hands up to stop him I would have to big scars down my face. I just felt like I had to fight the world He was like the devil .my mom finally got up come in the living room and seen me with all this bandage around my hand and cried Carrie what has happened . I told her I had to be at hospital at 9 am can she come with me I got stabbed. She sobbed and we returned back to hospital as soon as the hospital seen me they said I needed a operation on my hand has the tendons had been cut .they rushed me on a ward I don't remember much else apart from my mom sitting by my bed starring at me worried sick. After I had come round from operation all I remember hearing is Carrie who done this to you. Two police officers were standing in front of me questioning me. My hand so hurting now really bad ,they kept on and on ,I told them exactly what happened and told them his name , I didn't care he had no right to hurt me.

After a day they let me out my hand was fucked up for the year and it still is to this day. That p had waited for me as soon as I got to my mom's; he said we are going back to London tomorrow but needed some money for travel. My mom said she would see what she could do. He took me back to fire town and left me at his sisters flat, they didn't care just said we told you not to get mixed up with him. I looked out of the window and who did I see P and Tangus walking down the road together talking like they are best mates I couldn't believe it . I got out of the flat and went on the bus to my moms. I sat there just thinking of everything that was going on and before I knew it he was at the door. He said come we are going, I didn't want to I wanted to stay with my mom. She told him to take care of me and I just smiled I knew what was coming back out on the streets robbing. I wish I could get rid of this bastard everywhere I turn he is their I can't get away, my mom just wished us the best if only she knew what I was really going through then maybe, well .my hand was still throbbing from the cut I didn't realize that when you get stabbed you don't feel it but after the operation I was feeling it. He was just thinking about drugs all the way to London .I hated him so much ,he said we was going to a different part of London to raise some money I was scared and shaken by what had already happened to me I just didn't know what was going to happen next with this cunt he's crazy.

I just had to do as he said every minute of the day fear would run through my head none stop I would sit down and shake constantly and that bastard would kick the fuck out of me because it done his head in . We got a rented flat in Camber well green furnished. Yes it went ok for the first few weeks with the robbing I was taking people back to the flat and they were getting robbed. I was still hurt I still couldn't move my hand but I still did what I was told. One day we had a bad day no one was around to get robbed it was on top and the police was around. He got a paper from the shop and phoned a house clearance, he got them to come to the flat and empty it out for 250 pound. I knew this was going to be trouble he didn't care at all. Got the money went to Cold Harbor lane and brought a big stone. God all this was making me ill I had problems my head it would keep itching which is caused through stress, but the worst thing was that when P had smoked his drugs and I was left sitting their itching my head cause of the condition he would beat me up because he said I was making a sign for the police to come in and get him. What the fuck is he like, bastard, why was a 15 year old girl getting this stress I would just shout kill me, just fucking kill me, when he was beating me up, I had enough I wanted my life to be over if I was going to be living like this I would tense my body and hold the beatings and tell myself it didn't hurt. I had no contact with anyone I would phone my mom from time to time but I couldn't say what I wanted to because he was always with me. One night we was in the flat there was nothing in we was sitting around the gas fire on the floor he was smoking his shit and said that he's hungry cook some food . "How can I we got no cooker. I said "cook the fucking food on the fire "the more questions I asked the madder he got."Get the fucking fork and cook the food in the fire. I sat there with the sausage on a fork holding it in the fire and some planting in the other hand. I was burning my poor hand I still couldn't feel it properly through the stabbing I felt humiliated tears rolled down my face as we sat there for hours and I cooked this bastards food on a gas fire, we sat in the dark he would not let me put the light on he would hit me if I asked him to. He was so paranoid it was sending me mental I knew I couldn't take it all that kept running through my mind and my only escape route would be to kill him ,

I hated him anyway and he was going to kill me one of these days. When I think about it now I was 15 contemplating murder I would think of ways to do him in and how I would do it. Would I do it when he was a sleep or when he is high off the crack or what? I just didn't know and deep down I wanted another way out please I would cry to myself please someone help me. The cries went unheard and things just seemed to get worst and worst .It came on top at flat the landlord called police because of him selling the furniture we got locked up. Got interviewed and charged along with him. The social workers had to bail me out and that was it had court date and now nowhere to live. He was mad it wasn't my fault what do you expect if you rob someone's things. I 'm telling you now I just didn't know what was going to happen to me he was so controlling and such a bully I really did not deserve to be treated this way . We got another flat in Brixton close to Stretham hill where all the punters was. I was so messed up I just began to forget all the things that was happening and think of a safe place where I was alone without this cunt driving me mad and abusing me.

There was never a safe place with him but he was all I knew and being in a big city with no one to save me where could I go, back to my mom then he would be there soon enough to take me away again ,if I told my mom ,she would not have listened and as soon as he was at the door would hand me over just to save having trouble on the door . Because that's all I was to them trouble and I knew there was no point in even trying to get away. I would only make things worse for myself when he did catch up with me. I just done everything he said , I started to get very cheeky with him when he was off his head and I would hit him and kick him he would just sit there I would really lose my temper with him because I knew I could and get away with it he would get me back another day but I didn't care I hated him, the one night I punched him in the face totally forgetting I had stitches still in my left hand I hit him , I am left handed so it was natural I felt some pain in my hand blood coming through the bandage . I had only gone and knocked the stitches out my hand. Fuck this I am going to the hospital I am not sitting bleeding for hours like before. They couldn't restitch it so I had it heel funny my hand is fucked to this day. I had to try and get on with p because he was all I knew as much as I hated him. When I was waiting for punters I would sing to myself to take my mind off what was going on and to cheer myself up .I love music I always have .As a little girl I would dress up as Madonna and sing all her songs in the back garden, I'd wish I was doing that then only this time I would be another little girl and not Carrie so I would be tucked up in bed safe from these evil streets. No instead 2 am I'm walking the streets taking men back to rob.

He brought a car so he could sit in the car and watch me. Ha the fucker got locked up the feds said he's dodgy I got the car keys he told me to wait for him. I had never driven a car before in my life and now he was locked up what would I do.

The only thing I had been thinking of was getting to see my mom .I couldn't move the car for ages I had to ask someone to help. I took back to the garage where he got it from and asked to exchange for any car that was automatic , he did I got this yellow ford popular ,great I thought I'm heading straight for the motorway . I hadn't a clue what I was doing I just put my foot down and went. Was on m42 it was light when I had set out it was now dark , very dark this lorry was behind me all the way with his lights on full beam , I wondered why and why is he behind me like this ,I didn't care I was carrying on . It wasn't until I come off the motorway I flicked a switch and the car lit up. What I couldn't believe it I just drove down the m42 pitch black with no lights thank God that lorry was behind me. When I got to my mom's after a long mad trip in that car. She was at work so I drove to pick her up she said Carrie what you doing driving I got her in the car round some corners was on two wheels. She was pleased to see me and I was glad to be free for a while which soon ended. He was at my mom's after a few days back to square one. Round and round this viscous circle I go, straight back to London, he was mad because I had changed the car I didn't care anymore about anything. One night we was in a pub at Brixton and this man said to me hi don't I know you. P was mad he dragged me out the pub and beat me knocked my tooth out and even throw beer all over me. I just thought I don't know that man in the pub why is he doing this; he must know I don't know him. People would shout at him on street and tell him to leave me alone, and then he would get madder and start with them. He is driving me insane it's not fair why me. One night I got a man back to the flat and he came in "what the fuck you doing pussy boy" the same words every time he had a hat and sunglasses which he always wore to hide his ugly face, and this time the man only had 40 pound on him and bank cards he beat him and told him we are going to the bank. He got the man to take us to cash point in his car threatening him all the way, we was in the centre of London I remember just passing Brick lane and he pulled up at cash point and we all got out, the man run down the road screaming we run he told me to stay with him I tried to keep up with him but we was un aware we was running in to police who was looking for us. That was it got locked up this time I was not being let out got charged with kidnapping and robbery. I was told by p not to say anything in interview I didn't. They remanded me in to care again. At last maybe I would be safe for a while. They sent me to a home and the judge told them they must look after my every need I was going to be going on trail if I was pleading not guilty. Well I was safe he went to Bell marsh jail and I was in oxford in the middle of the field it was a lovely home and they showed me a bit of time of day and made sure I had everything I needed. I had no tooth so I had a gold tooth put in paid for by the home, I had clothes and shoes and food I felt like normal for once the house was a farm house and didn't feel like the other homes I had been in. they got a physiatrist in to see me because they thought I was having problems with my mind, well I was all the shit I had been through so far and I was a kid I was cracking up but didn't know what to do. My mom and little sister came to see me and I really enjoyed them seeing me living right for once. It didn't last long before I knew it I was sent to Surrey a kids home their closer to London because I was going to be on trail at have a guess which court , the Old Bailey crown court in central London .

I got to this new place and because I was so close to London I would jump on the train and go to the prison to see him. The trail started I felt lost in that court I remember sitting outside the court room looking at the machine what was used to cut people's heads off, which was on display in the court the walls were so tall with paintings on it was a beautiful building . It went on and on back and to court then one day the victim was in the wittiness box and we was all in court, the judge said can you describe the people who robbed you, and the man pointed at P in the dock well of course straight away p got released and all charges dropped because you cannot identify someone by pointing them out in the dock. P was happy he said it's my lucky day. I was still on the charge. I went back to kids home he told me to let him in my room so I did I sneaked him in and we got caught out , I ended up sleeping in a train station with him on a bridge freezing cold . I was turning 16 so I knew that I could get a flat. the home helped me to get one in crystal palace .I still had my case hanging over my head and didn't know what was going to happen but I know the judge told me I m going to prison for this so I was ready . I had a room in a house full of students it was dirty they had drugs and p kicked the door in and robbed them so I had to leave.

Went to Peck ham and had a proper rough time there to I never went to court so when I did finally get locked up I went straight for sentencing."As this offence is so serious you will do 12 months in jail to run with the other charges "the judge was very serious looking down his nose at me. Oh well I'm glad bye London I'm better off in jail. I lost touch with p for a few months then and got on with my bird I ended up in style a Manchester jail it was sweet there I had weed I was a cook and no one fucked me around.

I tell you there were some bitches in their some big fuck off monster bitches, and no one could get to them because they were protected because their crimes were so sick they would of got beat to death, so apart from that it was good. I made mates with some good Manchester girls and when the one got out she came to see me proper looked after me. I sailed through the bird P came to see me once before he got locked up again. He started writing and we got to have inter prison phone calls I was happy after our calls he would tell me he loves me and how much he missed me. It made me feel like someone cared about me and as much shit I had been through so far, it was behind me because I was too young to foolish to see how dangerous this man is. I thought he cared I just let go of the past and started to fall in love with him because I thought the way he was treating me was love .it was all I knew so what could I do. Any way when I got released from jail I went back to wolves I wanted to start a fresh and try and get a job I was never going back to London I hated the place, I got a little flat and got on well I had a job at a hotel and I was doing good .I was in touch with p waiting for him to come out of jail. He did and he messed up everything back on drugs, beating me sending me shop lifting again and I lost my job, he got me to a lowest point in my life ever but I was like a Muppet I was sucked in by him .it got so bad that we had nothing and living with an old man someone he knew, it was horrible and dirty it stunk like crap and made me feel sick.

one night he had just been in fire town with me and got us a lift from a guy who I went to school with and two other guys .the guy only had a mini and p made me sit in the front because he didn't want me sitting next to the guys in the back .driving along the road all I remember is a smash and I woke up next to a brick wall had just been throw the wind screen and I saw the three guys who was in the car running off down the road . I looked at myself and saw I didn't have one cut on me at all ,saw p he was knocked out in the back seat I wake him up to see if he was alright I said come on we got to get out of here ,it took me a few times to get him up he was mad when he come round we run from the car over a big park .he shouted "Where's the shit it's your fault" he kicked the shit out of me beat me up for hours over that park saying It was my fault I wanted to be lifted off the earth and saved that seemed like the only thing that could happen because this man was hurting me, and I saved him I cried out loud no one could hear I hated him again bad .he took me back to fire town to look for the guys to get some more crack . Ended up in the gambling house where men gamble and he was still kicking the fuck out of me in front of all these men I knew some of them, he kicked me hard in my belly time and time again un till one of the men in their smacked him in the face and knocked him out ,I will never forget he looked at me and said "go home to your mom ".he made sure I got out of their I run 6 miles all the way home to my mom. It took me about an hour when I got in have a guess who was sitting in the living room with my dad , yes P the bastard my mom was at work and he sat with my dad and talked as if nothing had happened I saw him and ran upstairs I sat in the corner of the room and covered my head with my hands he came in the bedroom and beat the fuck out of me again ,in my parents' house he hit me time and time again in my head I was so used to being beat now it didn't hurt ,or I tried to tell myself it didn't hurt . My dad never came up to help, my mom come back and caught him hitting me. I shouted I just was in a car crash I was bruised up real bad .she said we are going to hospital and then p started saying he has hurt his back, I hoped he had she got us in a taxi and we got checked out I was fine apart from I had lost a baby I didn't even know I was having. Straight away I thought bastard he kicked it out of me I hated him I just thanked God that I was still alive you know I was stuck with this cunt when he got out of hospital came to my mom's to get me and I was waved me off once more with this beast. He got locked up for robbery and got sent to Gloucester jail I went to see him and I moved over there got a bed and breakfast where the benefits would pay for the costs. I was lonely their but I made friends with a guy and his girlfriend and I felt a bit better.

It was funny because it s a lovely town and at bang up I could go and stand by the prison wall and shout to p , it was a small jail and I felt good because I had no bad thoughts around me it was a clean start . I made some more friends and felt happy I moved to a flat after a month of being there because I got the money together to get one. I was happy and loved my little flat I had more and more mates because I am very sociable and do get on with people it's just some times, well I do get in to a few argument but that is only because I know directly when someone is taking the piss and I'm on to them .with all the shit I had been through wasn't about to let no one mess with me. I keep things sweet and went to the jail to visit as often as I could, P said he wanted to marry me when I turned 18, I was infatuated with him by this time and thought of just marring him and having a family, he said he would change when he comes out and that things would be different, he would stop smoking drugs and look after me . Who was I fooling no one but myself how can he ever change he knows nothing but violence drugs and crime. He wanted to marry me on my 18 TH birthday ,he would still be in prison and that meant that I would get married and he would go back to jail .I thought about it and I said yes ,he said book register office and I did .I got myself a white suite and shoes my mates did my hair nice and they were witness to our marriage, it was weird because we both messed up on our words and he was standing in handcuffs and two prison guards at each side of him , what was I thinking I do not know. It was over quick and before I knew it he was gone, he told me to go to jail and see him because we could have a long visit. Not thinking I went straight to the jail and found myself sitting in the visit room with all the other visitor's in my wedding clothes and then out p comes he had got changed and didn't look happy . He said why I had come to see him in my wedding clothes why didn't I get changed. I was shattered I was his wife and he could only think about what I was wearing.

Well he made me feel so horrible on that visit and it was my birthday to, I was heartbroken because seeing him act like that towards me when we had just got married proved to me that he was not going to change at all. I had calls of mates they said we are going in to Cheltenham to party ,I didn't feel like it but I needed to take my mind of things so I went , and I had a real good night they all looked after me and I forgot about that cunt for a time. My mates must of thought I was mental to marry a criminal who was locked up, I didn't care they helped me though some hard times. My mom tried to tell me not to get married know member of my family come none of his come. I had to learn by my mistakes so I had to learn the hard way. He got out of jail and the day he did he was like a nuttier let lose just because a guy said hello to me by the shops he went mad on me, I run off and left the flat I had to wait till he was asleep before I could get away, when he was I went to my mates round the corner I asked her if I can stay for a while ,he didn't know exactly which flat she lived in but he knew where about it was. I was asleep on settee and I heard a shouting and beeping of car horn I heard him outside shouting his head off. I looked out the window he was stood in the middle of the road with only his underpants on ,I felt ashamed and went down he got me in the car and slept with one eye open .I couldn't believe how worst things were and I knew he was a mad bastard from I saw him with pants on looking for me . He told me I got to learn to drive so it was a long time since I drove that car from London and it was automatic I could not change the gears. He told me to get in the driving seat outside the flat and told me to drive the car I was stalling and I was very nerves so I couldn't focus then I felt a smack in my face "drive the fucking car now you are showing me up, and hit me again . I was nerves I just couldn't seem to drive the car I always seemed to make things worst especially when I was trembling this cunt would not let me get out the driving seat I had to drive the car , I hated him and I didn't want to learn to drive with him . As time went on he got more in to the drugs and I was suffering in his hands no one knew anything he was all the contact I had and when he let me call my mom he would stand there to make sure I didn't tell her anything. It finally came on top in Gloucester and we went back to Wolverhampton that's when we stayed at his sister's house and I found out I was pregnant.

I told you how things was when I was having my baby he would still make me go shoplifting and would only hit me in my face when I was pregnant I just kept going on and on with the same old bullshit I got locked up quite a lot and found myself in jail .at 19 pregnant and had pure messed up people around me I had a lot of outstanding charges and thought I could be in jail when I give birth. Travelling from Liverpool jail to Birmingham crown court being stuck in a sweat box and having nothing to eat all day ,not getting back to the jail till 7 at night and missing the dinner so I was banged up with nothing to eat and I had two to feed . On the way back to the cell I told the screw they just ignored me. Then I seen a loaf of bread coming through the hatch at least I had that. I didn't want to be in jail this time I just wanted to have my baby and be happy. Thankfully I got out and had my baby. All through this madness I kept my faith and just hoped that I would be strong. Well getting back to where I was after I had enough of everything and moved to Manchester. My God he was so envious of my mates because they were all helping me out with the baby and that they knew he was a cunt they could see how he was treating me .He found himself involved with the drug sense again and was going on mad ones robbing and that . I told him straight that I was not going to be shoplifting anymore.

One night we was invited to a party at one of my mates houses was all sitting there trying to enjoy ourselves and he was flirting with my mates mom, he came to me and said he will be back in awhile, any way he still hadn't come back and then there was a phone call p had been caught red handed with my mates t v in his hand robbing the house ,everyone looked at me I broke down I felt so ashamed these people are helping me out . That day I was sitting in my living room with my mates and he was robbing the house, well they stuck by me and knew I had nothing to do with it. We was sitting round my place my baby was in his basket by the front room window I heard him banging the door down he must of got out the police station on charges . I didn't let him in next thing I know a house brick came crashing through the window landed next to my son's basket all glass everywhere. My mates went and he came back I didn't have time to think but knew I had to move area and try again as much as my mates made me feel welcome and not to worry about what he did , I felt guilty and couldn't face them after a while so I moved from Oldham to Sal ford. In a gritty flat but I had to try and sort myself out hope this fucker don't mess up again. Well what can I say he got talking to a crack head girl who lived in the next block to us? She had a daughter who was 5, and would come round for him to get crack for her he would be only too happy to help her in that department, and have a lot out of it for getting it, he told me to look after her daughter. I sat their holding my son screwing because he was going to be trying his tricks now he's on the crack bad. Looked at the little girl who was so pretty and sweet but you can tell she was not looked after , "do you want some sweets "she was so hungry I fed her with chips and nuggets they got back , cracked off their head that bitch took her kid and he was left with me. I didn't say a word just knew that my son would never end up going without because his dads on drugs, I was going to make sure of that. Time went on and p got locked up again and got sent to strange ways , for robbery again , you know what when I knew he was in prison you know what I did I went to that girls flat who had the little girl and walked in the flat , the kid was not dressed and eating dry cornflakes . I had left my baby with this guy Alan who lived opposite me he was from Birmingham and we would chill together and have a drink. I grabbed the bitch out the flat shut the front door and kicked the fuck out of that slag, "look after your daughter" I told her.

It was different in Manchester I would walk down the street with my son and everyone would talk to me and say how sweet my son is, I loved it and got cozy. The kids would throw bricks at this man and tell me not to talk to him because he is a pedophile. The Jewish people was so different to us and it would amaze me how they live such an in closed life. That p sent some guy round to see me ,he had just got out of jail and was giving me some drugs to take to p .yes I had smuggled drugs in the prison before ,but strange ways was on top bad. The police would park outside and wait for someone to get caught and lock them up. I knew I had to be smart or else they would take my son off me. I wrapped and wrapped the drugs and went in with it in my mouth because I knew that I would have no choice but to shallow it if it got to hot. Well it did and the screws jumped us I swallowed the drugs the screw said I would have made sure if I had of got them drugs off you, that you would of gone to jail. I was glad I did what I thought was right it saved me and my poor baby. I had enough of risking my freedom for a cunt like him I was starting to get wiser to his tricks .He wasn't in to long before he was back out to bother me, that guy who lived by me in the flat had a big fight with him, cause I was throwing him out and he was pushing me around and shouting, Alan come in and hit him and they started fighting, I was glad he had helped me .but it didn't make things better just worst. He had got in touch with that guy who bought the drugs round for me to take to the prison. Now he was safe and I had his phone number and he had helped me with a situation when p was locked up. He took some drugs off him .the guy was looking for him and I was not about to be shot because of him so I got my things together and told him I'm going to live in Black pool. He come with me and treated me like shit I got a nice bedsit and he would spoil everything. The man kicked us out of there ,he said he don't agree with domestic violence I was beginning to get nasty back with p and I would fight him without a   second thought I think because of all the beatings he had already give me I got used to it and would give as much as I could take sometimes. I was fed up big time, I got a sea front bedsit it was horrible I hated it there and would go out on long walks down the beach with my son.

Would be thinking of how I would ever get rid of this fucker. I thought of everything but nothing seemed to help. Finally I broke and I went back to my home town wolves. I didn't want to but I had to do something was so lonely and p was trying his best to make things as bad as possible sometimes I would look at him and see red. I went to his sister's house the one I liked , she let us stay ,he would keep on and on telling me I got to go shoplifting and I would keep saying no . The one day he grabbed my son out his buggy and ran off up the road with him. I was scared what was he doing I ran up the road after him screaming give me my baby. Thank god a woman came out and got my baby off him and took me in her house. I was upset I really do mean

49

it when I say I hate him now because I did, I tried to go back to his sisters and he came back and took me to his mates house ,he told me that his mates girlfriend would watch my son and I could go with him on a raise. Well when he wanted drugs I had to do as he said because he was dangerous. He and his mate took me to the beat where girls sell their self .told me to get some money and they would be watching me so nothing would happen to me. Oh here we go day jar vu, I was mad he had no right to put me on the street and I am not going to jail again for robbery. You know what I did, I got in the first car that stopped and told him to take me to where my son was. I left the man outside and told the girlfriend to give me my baby and I ran out the back door with my son , luckily enough I knew this girl who lived in the next street to them and I knocked her up it was after 12 in the night , the girl still lived with her mom . She let us in and let us sleep the night , I was awake most of the night I just felt weird .watched my little boy sleeping all snuggled up , I heard his voice I'm sure I did I knew he didn't know about my mate who lives here I knew we was safe. I thought about everything this man had put me through since the age of 15 and made a decision to get away from him, I wanted a divorce I was not his wife I never really have been and I never will. I was going to change my life and stay out the way just me and my baby. I went to a hostel the next day and settled in with my son it was the only thing I can do to get us a house and be away from all the rubbish that was surrounding me and   my son . I was hurt and I wanted to hurt p even though I was out the way and he didn't know where I was, I called the guy from Manchester who p had taken drugs off .I told him what he had done to me and where he could find him, he said he was going to get some guys from this way to deal with him, and told me not to worry about him.

I heard through the grapevine that p got battered and now the police have locked him up for robbery.

I was glad he got a good beating before he got locked up , I didn't know whether it was anything to do with the call I made , I didn't care he was off the street and had a taste of his own medicine . Time went on and I got through to a lawyer about a divorce as I was still married I wanted nothing to do with this mad man again once that paper was here I would be me again. I got myself a place after a lot of stress with the council p wrote letters to my mom's house I would read them and I had to tell him that he has got to sign the paper for divorce ,he said he wouldn't unless I take Ty to see him. I did go to the jail Winston green bang up jail. Was in the visit centre and he didn't even say anything apart from please just bring me some drugs .what got me mad was that he didn't even look at my son he was going on and on and on. I had my sons toy wresting figure with me I was angry I got up throw the toy in his head it smacked off his fore head and cut his head , I throw the chairs and got to the door to leave ,"you bastard you won't fuck with me anymore ".the screw let me out , he was laughing saying you soon told him good on you , I took a last look at him blood ran down his face I was glad I had such a good shot when I was angry ,that's nothing if you mess with my head now I'm thinking clear ,I will take yours off cunt. It finally came through I was free , I was not a crack heads wife any more ,I was not a lost little girl any more I knew what I wanted and I was focusing on getting a good life for me and my boy. We have been through so much with different things that had happened I had to find some light and as much as my son's dad produced a lovely little boy. He would never be a dad to Tyrone he didn't have it in him, and a dad would not think about drugs before his own son, it was so clear that from the day my baby was born all he was interested in was himself, I'm going to be a bitch from now on I know how his mind works I'm going to think about number one. My baby and me and what a lovely little boy he is, he bought me so much joy and I thank God so much for blessing me with my son. Because he is mine and I will always treasure him. I think now this chapter comes to a close I got rid of my sons dad and I was moving on and I had time to grow up I was free I have ambitions I want to make my son proud of his mom I don't want to be a bad role model …I'm a changed girl I'm going to leave the past behind and turn the page.

CHAPTER FOUR
LOOKING UP......

I was doing well me and my son had a house down by my mom she was helping me and I was happy. I started to go out and socialize with people again and my son was growing up beautifully. I was under pressure had no money but I still tried to make the most of things. One night I was out at a night club in Birmingham and a man asked me if I was a dancer ,I had my short dress and heels on and for one time in my life felt sexy like a women . "What do you mean dancer". he said "a lap dancer because you look like one , I let it blow over my head and said no . I forgot about what he said and got on with things, one day I bought the paper and saw a job advert for lap dancers in a club in city centre. Umm I thought that man had said I look like a dancer but I had never done anything like that before and me being me was inquisitive .I phoned the number and was told to attend a interview and to bring a long dress and out fits to change in to . I was excited I got a nice long dress from town and shoes on and got the train to the interview. I got in the club, it was nice and posh I liked it I meet the manager ,he was very nice he shook my hand and looked at me told me to get changed and start working . I thought to myself well it's now or never and even if I didn't know how to pole dance I'm sure to have to learn . I didn't know anything about dancing or even what it was all about. There was lots of girls in the changing room and I just got on with it , when the club opened the men came in we all had working interview's which meant that we was left to work and would be called to the stage through out the night and would be watched to see how we did. I soon got talking to other girls and found out what I could do to help me out. The night went ok and I was asked to come back to work the next night, in which I did and I carried on working and getting better at dancing and making money .the first night I made 100 pound just over , I was happy the first time on the stage I was very nervous and I watched the girls on pole before me and copied what they was doing in a not so obvious way. I couldn't do tricks but didn't do too bad. The months went on and I was getting better and better at the job and making a lot more money I was feeling great, because of my past I don't really talk too much .I went to the club to work not make friends and would focus on talking only to the men.

I would say hello and I had my set of mates, but there was a lot of bitchy vibes because the competition and jealousy because another girl is more popular than the rest. Well 2 years went on I worked 3 nights a week and was on at least a grand a week easy. I worked my way to the top and was number 1, as the boss would say "you are my f1 why isn't every girl like you."

I got really good at dancing and was number 1 in the club, the girls didn't like it but what could they say to a girl like me. I had so much fun and was a really entertaining performer I loved it I felt so sexy and the men loved it. I had my own character and everyone would ask me how I do so well , I just be myself , I said giving nothing away, I would spend 200 pound on one pair of jeans and waste money like there was no tomorrow. I would just think to myself I will make at least 300 tomorrow it doesn't matter. Me and my son was doing really well I got so much joke at work we had money for once and things were looking up. The past started to seem so far behind us now and I hadn't seen p for at least a few yrs. I had good mates and wasn't worrying about anything. I started having driving lessons and would catch the train to Birmingham and get a taxi back, there was always a drama every night at work and I would enjoy the excitement it took my mind of things, all these men throwing money at you for dancing to one song, yes I got my tits out and they knew about it when I did. I had good custom that would spend an hour talking to me and give me 300 pound for that I lapped it all up. I done the job for 8 years so you can imagine that there is way too much to mention apart from some of the highlights. Like one day I was late and nearly missed the train to the city , just jumped on in time looked up and there was at least 30 Bristol city fans on the train , I just walked past and sat down I thought yes I will sit here and smoke my joint because I know the ticket man is not coming round when fans are on the train, sitting their minding my own business smoking some of the guys came and talked to me "where you of " I thought here we go ."To a special place want to come," thought I would wind them up. "can we have some of that joint" I said yes but I will only leave you the last few pulls ,so there I was smoking down the weed and I didn't like to share a joint I had a long night a head I needed to be chilled to entertain .I thought to myself what the fuck I stood up we was just 5 min away from my stop any way cut a long story short I was getting chatted up and I said to the guys get some money together right here and now and I will show you what sort of club I'm going to. They did I had about 40 pound I held on to the rail on the train and started swinging round the pole and dancing so sexy in front of all these guys and down the back of the train was normal people like old men and woman .they was going wild when I started dancing they loved it just before the train stopped I grabbed one of the men and got my tits out and shoved his face in between my boobs. . That was it I was getting off the train, they was singing to me "we love you Brumie's we do we love you Brumies we do" and cheering. I was laughing my head off how can I be so mad to do that, but that's just it that's the kind of crazy person I am and I love it really,

I am not an attention seeker, but I do get noticed. I was saving for a car I had a few grand and like I said was wasting money I paid 700 pound for a chain that was so big it was un real .it was very nice though. I was on cloud nine for a time and loving the fact I was free and me and my son was doing ok. Because I knew what hard really was having to rob or steel all my life that's in the past I would never do anything like that again, it is not just because I have money now either because I stopped long before now. But all I would like to say is to the people who did get caught up in the madness of me when I was a teen that I am sorry and if I know now what I should of understood then, things would have been different, and I'm sure that everyone has forgot about me now, going back to the point I was living good and my son what's mine is his and that's how it will always be. I did think of writing music and I wrote some songs and had an idea what beats I wanted and I had the money so I booked sessions at the studio. I have always been told I am good with words and that's why I was doing so well at dancing to because I could talk the talk and walk the walk, this was my little secret and it was the key to dancing because you could be as pretty as Pamela Anderson if you have not got no talk then their is not no point in walking. And I produced wrote and sang two kind of garage tracks and I was setting my sights higher I wanted to do more and more and wrote other tacks but have not done anything with them. I listened to the tune s the other day and I did laugh and say what was I thinking , but this is the point at that time in life I was thinking of dancing making money and listening to it told me a story and I was proud .

The one track called higher, which is a sort of one word tune which I thought of one off the nights I couldn't sleep. I know it sounds mad but with the beat the word higher sang nicely sounds good , I added a few words in the verses and I like that tune the best .and yes I had taken an e got in bed tried to sleep and I couldn't stop myself singing ,,"higher higher and higher and higher." I was enjoying myself I had men who would give me their last dime just for me to dance for them and I had been seeing one guy on and off. He was good in bed totally and he was a big flirt so it was just like that and he did work in the lap dancing club with us. I didn't want a relationship any way so I just wasn't at all bothered because I was happy being single. Before I go on about the tunes I cut. I did nothing with it when I had finished I was to wrapped up in the dancing thought I was trying to float a sunken ship so I put the CD away in a bag and forgot about it. My little sister or my mom would baby sit for me when I was out, for once I didn't feel like I wanted to run away from anything, because I feel like my whole life I have been running, from police evil people, something or other I never felt more settled before and was glad things were finally starting to look up. I have got a good heart and would always be there for my family and friends because I am a loyal and honest person. It took me some time to understand my own mind but once I did I was fine I knew how to reverse the psychiatry to get what I wanted out of life. Only I didn't have the chance to think for myself all those years I was with that bastard and I know it sounds bad to keep calling my sons dad a bastard but this is my book and I'm writing how I feel and how it is and how it will always be in his case ,because deep down to me that's all he is a dirty bastard he would still write the odd letter to my mom's house which I would just flick throw and throw it in the bin I wasn't interested , that was the last chapter I had no intentions of getting in touch with him. I just want to be worry free from now on and if something is worrying me I will just deal with it calmly I was even beginning to learn how to cope with my temper and I was good   .

I was looking after myself nice I had a gym membership and would do my hair get a tan and to be honest I was turning in to a sexy young women I had so much confidence I didn't know where it was coming from but I was glad . That is what you really need in life to get any where no matter what you want to do or how hard it seems. All you need is confidence in yourself and you will get through. As I said about getting a tan one day I had just finished and was leaving the salon and seen a man I hadn't seen for years, he used to sell weed and that's all I knew ,he was from fire town "hello "as our eyes caught each other. "oh hello how are you" we got in to a little chat and he mentioned about when I got stabbed throw the hand in fire town , he said that pussy who done it was a wanker. We exchanged numbers. I hadn't even brushed my hair that day and I was rushing off. I didn't think anything of it got on with things. Well this is the case, I just don't think sometimes. Maybe if I had off listened in the first place I would not have had to go through most of the stuff I did.

CHAPTER FIVE
ON A LEVEL...

The guy who I give my number to was on my case he would call and want to meet me and say nice things. I will call him 50. I don't want to mention his name for many reasons. Yes things were looking hot with me and 50 and I was infatuated by him I liked him and it wasn't long before he was sleeping over every night of the week. He knew I was a lap dancer and didn't mind. He would wait up for me or be out and come back to me just before I got home. He would be on a level and I would tell him about a few funny things that happened that night I would have a bath and we would go to bed. He always seemed a bit quite but he said it's just him. He's always like it , the one day we spent the whole day just looking in to each other's eyes and holding each other I thought I was beginning to fall in love .After a few months well he was ok and I did enjoy having a man around me. There was a man who lived a few doors away from me who sold weed. 50 knew I bought weed from him and told me not to get none off him, well one day 50 was gone all day I wanted a joint so I went to the house to get some weed thinking nothing of it. When 50 did get back I didn't know where he had been and he always seemed to have a long bath when he got in , he asked where I got weed from , I told him and the next thing I know I have felt a big smack across my face .he had hit me and I couldn't believe it , I got my son and ran down the road and sat on the field with my little boy. Crying why he has done that, I couldn't believe it .I knew from then that he was just like p.

I didn't want to go back then surely enough 50 came walking to the fields and said he was sorry for hitting me. I was still easily sucked in when it came to men I was, went home and forgot it just got on with things. He seemed to be ok with me he did no I was a lap dancer and that I had a lot of trouble in the past with Tyrone's dad. He always seemed on edge and then one day I called him and he didn't answer the phone .I would leave a silly message like, why aren't you answering the phone .he would come back in a bad mood and I said why are you so quite ,he said he is always like it. He has been the same all along I would brush it off. I thought he was my man as every night no matter what he would end up with me. He even would bring his children for me to luck after .The one day I was looking after them one of the children said "daddy's got a new girl friend ".I was so angry I got on the phone and went mad "how can you have another girlfriend and you are living with me". He just said wait till I get back. Oh I was so upset, why does everyone just want to hurt me .well he got back took his children home come back to me and my son, he beat the crap out of me smashed my face of floor and cut my nose open. In front of my son, I was in a bad way .then after he beat me in front of my son he changed and started to clean the blood off my face saying he was sorry. But I knew this had been brewing for a while as he was out from 9 in the morning and would not be back till 8 in the night sometimes later. I knew what he was doing; he was seeing other women in the day and the nights I was at work and then act like I was the only one.

How could he want to hurt me and be so guilty himself? He brushed my hair for me after I had a bath to make me feel better. By brushing my hair like that ,I knew he was a nuttier as P had used to do that to me after he had beat me to , so I knew all the signs were there.

But I just felt trapped again. I was actually more scared of 50 then P. he just seemed to be so over powering no matter what I would say or do I could never win. Things started to get worst to I was getting beat up at least 3 nights out of the week by him. And it seemed like he wanted to do is hurt me he would make any excuse to lash out at me no matter where I was ,who was around he didn't care as long as it wasn't his kids. I knew he didn't love me because if you love somebody you don't treat them like that. If I was a bit late home from work he would hit me and say I'm shagging the boss of the club, he would tell me I was ugly and try to bring me down . He ripped my hair out so many times my head would hurt all the time. I knew it was only a matter of time I had to get away from him I could not be treated like this. I would go to work with my bruised body just to get out the house and away from him. People wanted to hurt him they didn't like what he was doing to me. I just carried on I would come home he would say how much money you made , I would say like 400 ,500 pound ,he would go mad and say "how the fuck can you make that much in a few hours work ". He hated the fact that I was so confident and strong no one could pull me down. He would shout at me right up close to my ears while hitting me. One night he just about took me out to a club, I didn't enjoy it at all I felt on edge I couldn't relax and enjoy myself. On the way back waiting for the train he was moaning and being nasty to me,

I wouldn't say much to him because he would hit me even more. I didn't say anything this time just standing waiting for the train, he smacks me in the mouth and my front tooth broke off. My lip was bleeding and all he kept saying is that I had made him do it. I cried all the way home on train he was telling me to shut up. But really I just couldn't stop the tears from falling, he was like a jackal and hide he would lash out at me and then when he realized what he had done to me, he would try and hold me and cry he is sorry.

I was beginning to feel really down now and I was becoming more and more drawn in to myself, would lock myself away and just go to work and wait for the beatings. My son was really insecure and he didn't care if he hit or shouted at me in front of him, he wouldn't do it in front of his kids .I felt so sorry for my son he was so scared I just knew I had to get away from him ,if not for me for my boy. Time went on and he just wouldn't stop he was horrible I felt like I was going mad at times he would try to brain wash me and tell me that all the time he hits me it's my fault, I would just agree. I really did not know how much more of this bastard I could take. Sometimes he would lock me out my own house if I was a little late from work I would bang down the door I knew he could hear me. I remember sitting in the alley round the side of my house crying and praying to God that things will change and praying he wouldn't hurt me when he finally lets me in. because I knew he was going to, that was why he locked me out so he can start again for nothing . I had to use my head I had to be strong I had to try to outsmart him he was too dangerous to mess about with .I had to always agree with him and let him think he was right to do what he was doing to me. No one on this planet deserves to be treated the way that evil cunt treated me .I put up with it for so many years when I should of got away long before I did . I was silly and should have learnt by my first mistake with P, it's easy to say things but doing them is two different things. I have now learnt if I say I'm going to do something I will do it no two ways about it ,life is too short to be waiting around and being surrounded by negative people. I had to try and keep him sweet the best of times to make my life easier.

We went on holiday together to turkey. Well he had told me that he was going to change and wouldn't hit me , how long did it last not long in turkey he kicked the shit out of me and dragged me across the floor cutting all my legs .I hated him I hated the holiday and just couldn't wait to get back to England . My family at this stage had drifted off again ,and said if I didn't leave him they would not talk to me again ,it was easier said than done he was so obsessed with me I think he actually got a high off hurting me . I was just back to the old times when I had a evil man hurting me and telling me what to do , why did he want to bring me down he couldn't stand the fact that I could do whatever I wanted to and I could make money and look after myself . I tried my best to act as if I was alright at work but everyone knew I wasn't and could see most of the time the marks what he had left on me. I had people who wanted to hurt him and I didn't let it happen. We was on and off because of the beatings and I would call the police but never follow through with the charges. I loved my job and no man no matter how many beatings he wants to give me is going to stop me going. I didn't want to let him win he wanted me to be down in the gutter like he was.

I found comfort in a nice guy he was a D J and would tell me to leave him all the time, I enjoyed being with this guy but knew we would never have a full on relationship together he was too much of a flirt , but I didn't mind he cheered me up anyway in many ways. I was still making lots of money and 50 was following me he would wait to see if he would see me and try and talk to me .well the sorry worked again and mad me I let him back in to our life. I was still getting calls from other men because we was apart for at least two months. One night I got in from work and my phone rang, he answered it and it was a man .he instantly hung up I had a thick gold chain that I wore all the time he ripped it off my neck and beat me up bad with the chain. I couldn't even talk myself out of it. I would scream I wanted someone to hear me I wanted someone to help me but no one ever came. My poor little boy had to witness the abuse of this man and it wasn't right at all. Well time went on pure sadness and pain off this man I just don't know what I was thinking why I put up with it not once but twice. I had give up and it was starting to show ,my mates would ask if I was ok and if they could help me but all I wanted is to be away from these beatings and all this shit this bastard is putting me and my little boy through .

He cut all my designer jeans up and through all my clothes out he was a proper nasty piece of work. I was so scared of him one night I had finished work was in a taxi me and a mate on the way home and I spotted a white van ,I said to my mate it's the man who lives opposite me why is he following me. I was puzzled when I got home 50 was up in a bad mood,"what the fuck are you doing with that man over the road"I said what I just noticed him tonight on the way home". He hit me with the gym bar and shouted it's been going on for ages he always goes out the same time as you and comes back 5 minutes before you; he hurt me bad that night I had to get out of the house. I managed to jump out of the window because he had locked the door and taken the keys out. I could feel my check bone hurting it was swollen up and my ribs were hurting badly. I was in a mess I had to go to my mates I couldn't pick my son up looking like this .I got their and she said I got to stay with her until I sort myself out.

It took a few weeks to get back to normal as I was hurting for weeks all over .I couldn't even go dancing I was going to get a house out of the area and try again. He was hunting high and low for me but this time I said I am not going back he could of killed me and I can't take that chance again I got to be here for my little boy I am all he has. I started looking but I enjoyed living with my mate we would have a laugh all the time she did the same job as me and was on my level and would you believe its sherry my best mate now who I meet through the job. She's a proper mate and always will be. But I took my time I went back to seeing the D J now and then he did work at the club so it was hard not to ,I liked him. I would have a laugh at work and all the customers would enjoy my company and enjoyed me dancing for them. Yes there was a lot of hating and I brushed all the bitches off as they knew if they had a problem with me they couldn't do a thing about it unless they came to my face and told me and not one of them ever did. I went to work and that's what I did work hard and make some hard cash , I was rolling I passed my driving test first time I was really proud of myself and the next day I brought myself a car . It was nice a rover tomcat. It was sweet no more taxis no more walking I'm on the road and I was happy. I just couldn't believe that I had finally got a car and I'm free I haven't got to deal with little bastards who want to hurt me and bring me down no more. That 50 sent his brother in the club one night and he asked if he could talk to me , I just said ok he told me that his brother don't mean to hurt me it's just a problem he has got and that he is really upset and won't come out of his sister's house , he said he missed me. I just said ok. I knew he was not a liar as he had no need to but I forgot about that I was too indulged in getting my life on track. Trying to anyway.

I got a house it was big and it was in an area I didn't know but I took it and got stuff in there .was only in their a week and one night the electric cut off and as I was walking through the living room to turn it back on I felt really weird like their a strange atmosphere, just before I got to the electric box, it came back on and in the corner of my eye I could see a mist. I was scared and didn't like the house after that happened I had a holiday booked and was flying out to Lanzorote the next week, I just held it down and slept with all the lights on, I hated the house and I should of realized that on the day I went to view the property I bumped my car on the wall on the drive to the house, that was a sign to not move in but I ignored it.

I went on my holiday with my mom and family as we were talking again now and was getting on. Had a great holiday apart from my mom not liking the fact that no matter where I was I would get a lot of male attention. I couldn't help it. She said I was a slag and told my little sister that she had better not turn out like me .I wasn't a slag I just wanted to have fun and couldn't help it if I had some attention off people. I was pissed off so I got talking to a guy from London and went to his viler for a drink; he was too interested in snorting his coke so I chilled out. I knew we was flying home the morning and I knew I was going to have to leave this guy somewhere, once I was back at the apartments. It was 5 am and I told him I was ready to go back and get my key and then come back to the viler with him. He got us a taxi my mom had locked me out of the apartment and I had to get in. I asked the guy to give me a footy over a 10 foot wall , I pulled myself up and jumped down , right I could bang the door down now to get in as I couldn't get to it before, I got in , in the end and left the guy waiting. Don't know how long for but I'm sure he got the message. As soon as we landed in Birmingham I turned my phone on and listened to my voice mail. I heard "Carrie this is the police you need to get in touch with us, your house has been robbed". I was upset big time went back to the house everything had been taken even my settees I just couldn't believe it. I got what I could clothes and that and went to my moms. I needed some where safe I can't keep moving I had to settle down I knew living at my parents would be hard but not as tough as this shit I have been going through.

I got on with the council list and was waiting for a flat off them by my moms .it was good because my sister would watch my son and I would be making money and going out. I was back on with the d j and was having fun. It was too small at my mom's me and my son shared a bedroom with my sister. I needed space I couldn't wait to get my flat, but being back in the area I bumped in to 50. He stood in the middle of the road and I nearly run him over , I felt bad so I stopped he was pleased to see me and was telling me how sorry he was and how he had been waiting to see me round by my mom's house . We went for a drink and that together and he said he wanted to get back with me and he swore he would never ever hit me again. I said we will see and left it at that, sure enough he was always texting and saying he wanted to meet up, I was with the d j one night and he would not stop ringing me, I just through the phone down. Well I could not settle and ended up going back to wolves, I called him back he said he wanted to see me, so I went it was 4 am and he was at his sisters but she wasn't in. I just don't know what is wrong with my head sometimes, how can I go to spend time with a cunt who beat the shit out of me time and time again, well it's like I forgot and we slept together I felt weird because I was with the d j before him I did not expect it and he was holding me tight saying he loved me. I was a fool I'll admit but at the end of the day you only learn from your mistakes and that is the truth. My mom would go mad if she knows I'm with 50 again I had to try and keep it quite. But she knew something was going in the end and we fell out again, I can't blame her she didn't want to see me get hurt again. I moved out and went to stay with my mate again I was getting flat in a month so I knew it wouldn't be long. 50 was saying he was going to treat me right when I get my flat , a leopard never changes its spots and that is one saying I will always remember , no matter how long they keep the act of not wanting to hurt you .

They will hurt you in different ways as I found out. Time went on and I moved in and got the flat looking really nice for me and my son my mate helped me. Then 50 would come round and spend a lot of time just sitting around in my flat. I put up with it as I still was unsure of how long it would be before he blew up again. I was still dancing and he was just so quite I would say to him "why are you so quite ". he would keep saying I'm always the same , it really started to get on top of me and I was getting stressed out with this man in my face all the time just sitting around . Sometimes he would not wash or brush his teeth for days and I could smell the smelly bastard. I told him to sort his self out but he would just go off and start acting funny. I knew he wanted to hit me but he wouldn't, I just got down and depressed he would try and tell me how to bring up my son and at this stage my mates got pissed off with me because I had changed and didn't want to go out to have fun, they all stayed out the way, they knew what he had done to me before and told me to be careful. I was losing touch with everything and everyone was just sucked in again like a silly bitch, he was playing mental games with my mind, I knew he was mad by the way he would act and react to things. I hated him he got me so depressed I thought I was going to crack up. When he would get mad he would shout right up close to my ear and say "I'm too good for you, you are nothing". I would cry that's all I could do he was making mine and my little boys life such a misery I was going off the rails. I went off one day and booked a holiday for me and my son I didn't tell him until a few days we was going , he was mad but what could he do the next time he hurt me I was going to lock him up and he knew it. I was happy it seemed like going on holiday was my only escape from this cunt , he hated the fact that I was able to go and do whatever

I wanted while that numb skull as Tupac would say , was sitting around with a t v control in his hands watching t v documentaries about people getting murdered .it would scare me why he would want to sit in day in and day out and watch this crap ,it was like he was obsessed with it ,I would fear for me and my son I felt like I had to sleep with one eye open. He was a smelly cunt and he didn't care about me and my little boy he just wanted to bring me down and out like him. I was so determined to not let him win and get the better of me, I knew I had to hold it together but it was only a matter of time before it would get ugly.

The night before we was leaving to go on holiday he took my pass port off me .I went mad I kicked off and we had a big fight the fucker only strangled me with the towel I had round my body I had just got out the bath and he just had to start , well that was it I thought I am not going to make it my baby was a sleep well I say baby but my son was growing up now he was 8 when we went to Cyprus for the first time .I was going if it was the last thing I do , it got bad and one of the neighbors called the police because he really went to town on me that night, it's like all the anger had built up inside him and he just wanted to hurt me , the police came and I asked if they would just get him away from me and my son . I didn't want to press charges I just wanted to go on holiday. They did as I asked and I was glad I thought fuck you I will lock you up next time I couldn't breathe when he strangled me all I was thinking of was my son and how he would cope if this cunt done me in . I was scared at times I felt like he would kill me with his bare hands.

We went on holiday and had the time of our life, meet new mates my son loved it I could see how much better we was without that tramp around us, I just hoped he would leave us alone now. We had so much fun I didn't want to come back my son told me he hates 50 and can't forget what he did to me when he was a baby. I was very upset that my

little boy had to see all this and was going to start a fresh;
I was going to move without telling him. I had stopped
dancing now after 8 years of it I got fed up with it in the
end and needed to move on I had what I wanted out of
it even if I did waste a lot of it. I started my own business
.something that had no initial pay out. So I thought of a
cleaning business and got it in the yellow pages and on yell
and the calls started to flood in. I had lots of work on I
would work all day until my son finished school I think I
need to be at home when Tyrone finishes school as I love
my son and want to make sure he has all he needs , and that
is what he needs a good mom who is going to be there for
him . 50 got back in the flat I came back from work one day
and he was waiting in the hall way, I just let him in I knew
what I had in mind and just kept the peace. He had a lot of
family trouble like really bad and he needed someone to talk
to. I was there I tried to help him I'm far from bad minded
and was really trying to help him. He just started staying
again and then he stated taking things out on me, he would
switch on me for no reason and be really nasty to me I just
couldn't take it I had to get away fast. I had money so I was
looking for the right property close to my son's school. It
seemed like it was taking forever. The thought of going back
to the flat would make me feel sick, I didn't go out and I had
this man trying to blame me for everything that was going
wrong in his life. When he would call me on the phone
to see when I was coming back I would feel like I want to
smash the phone up I would start driving mad and get angry
.why I ask myself did I have to put myself through so much
crap time and time again knowing that really I'm only a
fool to myself to even think for one minute that 50 had any
love or feelings for me and my son is beyond me. But what
I do know is that if you have a strong mind and can pull
yourself out of the fire , when you do look back you will see
like me the true meaning of life . And that is not to allow

anyone ever take their hand to you and hit you because once they do they will never stop. They turn things around and try to blame you for the fights and I was even mad enough to go along with it and say "I know I'm sorry, it's my fault". Hoping and praying all the time that there has got to be a way out, it just seemed never ending. On and on I let myself go big time I put loads of weight on went to a size 16 I'm normally a 12 .

So I was at the end of the road and just waiting for the right time to get out of this madness. You know dancing for so long I really got to understand the way a man's mind works, it's like I could read his mind. He would hate it but I have got a gift that allows me to read in to things before they arise. But I can't stop them happening only wish I could. I was so low one day I felt like I was losing my mind and all I would do is work and get home and stay with my son in the bedroom while he was watching TV. One day he went out I sent my son to the shop for a newspaper he didn't want to go ,I shouted at him and said he must go to the shop , I couldn't go outside I was a mess . He went bless him and got me the paper as soon as he got in from shop I had the paper open on the property page. I looked down the page"please ,please let there be one ", didn't see none then I looked again , a house was in their the area I wanted , I called up straight away. I got a viewing and couldn't wait, so I drove past the house to see it…and what a shock I got.

As soon as I saw the house I knew that this is going to be the one I prayed that I would be able to get this house and sensed a good vibe from the first time I seen it driving past. I had never felt like that about any property I had to get it. Through all the pain blood sweat and tears me and my little boy had been through it was time we had a good fresh start. I went to see a physic lady before I had even got the number to the house. She told me some things that I knew she had no way of knowing it was the first time I had seen anyone like this. She told me that I would get a house and I would leave this man who has been so horrible to me. I had a few messages from beyond to and knew that she was for real. I did not for one minute think that she would be totally right about the house.

And do you know all through this trouble with 50 me and my son looked after my great uncle and great Aunty who was 91 and 89. I helped them as much as I could and so did my mom, and that is how we got talking to each other again. We went through so much and it was a shame to see how they had been married for 65 years still so much in love, it was sad to see my uncle bless him slip away, my aunt was ill had a heart attack and it took 2 years to get her back right, she is now in a good care home after going through a lot of trouble with care homes not looking after her properly. She is lovely Bless her and I will always find time to take her out shopping or to the park she is an inspiration. So was my great uncle Norman my son really looked up to him because he was in the r a f world war 2 and would tell him stories and show him the photos which we still have .I would always make my uncle laugh , one day I was alone with Norman and I went on the balcony for a smoke .the door shut and locked ,I had just sat my uncle down with his dinner , he had Parkinson bad and bless it took him about an hour to open the door he was laughing , I felt bad because it was so hard for the man to even get up never mind have to try and open the door I felt like a right idiot. He would always like the food I had cooked for them I honored him and my Arunt. I really started to see how much of a nice lady I was and how big my heart was because I hadn't known Norman and Thelma only seen them a few times and I was with my Nan shopping was a quick hello and good bye .I must of always been like this but not been able to show it because of how people have treated me. I won't trust another man so easy and will enjoy being single for a while the next man

I meet I need to know he is a good person and he needs to treat me the way I would expect a man to treat the women he loves. So the question is will I ever meet any one who suits my needs , hopefully yes I want to one day I don't want to be lonely .there is someone for everyone or so they say , we will see......

CHAPTER SIX
NO LOOKING BACK...

Yes to our surprise the house was perfect brand new house nice garden and we could move in within four weeks. I wanted the house had visions of me and my son sitting and chilling out together with no trouble at last. I did what I had to do to get the house signed over to me, I didn't tell 5o. I knew I would have to get out of the flat without him knowing. I went on as if nothing was going on I couldn't wait to be away from the stress .I had planed everything carefully and had things ready to just take , time went on and he kept asking me what I was up to and if I had another man. I told him no and tried to keep things quite about the move. One night he went out a few days before I was going to be moving in I had the keys and was on the sly taking things to the house I went back one night to get some more stuff ,I had left my son at my moms and said I would be back in a bit. Got in the flat he was in their sitting in the dark I turned the light on I knew this was it he was going to kick off. "what you doing here" he looked at me with those evil eyes and grabbed me "you fucking moving out bitch, you got a new man, take me to the fucking house now "he grabbed my phone off me and grabbed my hair, I was screaming he was going to do me in. "I will go to jail for you tonight" looking down my phone to see who I had been calling slapping me in my face. "you bitch you are going to show me the house now take me right now" no I said he throw the phone at me and I was screaming he went to the window to look out and told me to shut up, by this time I had called my mom and left the phone on so she could hear what was going on and call the police. He hit me and was trying to force me to tell him I had another man. I hadn't I just wanted to get away from him, he kicked me around I was screaming loud so my mom would hear on the phone and finally the buzzer went I ran to it. My mom and the police I was so glad to see them, "I heard everything it's a good job you did what you did with the phone, or he would have killed you". The police told him to go I yet again said I don't want to press charges I just want them to stay with me while I grab some things and go. And that is exactly what I did never looked back just knew that this is the end.

The end of people treating me like I'm dirt and as soon as I left that place I have been a changed person. Going when I did was just the right time I was on the edge and now I'm free and it feels so good. I am never going to let myself be so foolish again , I'm wise to a lot of things and no that the life I was living on the streets so to speak just wasn't right for me for any teenager . People moan and groan about what they haven't got and ponder on other peoples movements. What they are failing to see is that the most valuable thing they have is life and how grateful they should be that they are living. I see that through all my troubles I had and how many times my life could have been taken away from me. I thank God for helping me overcome the pain and strife. It's made me so tough and strong minded that it would be really hard to try to get inside my head. I think so much about different things I try to block out the past and me actually writing this book will be the last of it because I'm never going to dwell on the past. I live for the future and ways of making our life's better .It's been one long hard struggle and through it all my son kept me believing in myself, that I would get out of the fire and find a meaning to life instead of abuse and stress at the hands of another person. My son did not deserve to go through anything like that. I have seen such a big change in him now ever since we moved he is a changed boy. I can just see how much of a lovely little boy he is and it hurt him to see how much I got hurt as young as he was when it started happening. It is totally wrong of me to keep him in such an environment and he will never forget he used to have nightmares and it took me a long time to ensure him that nothing was going to happen to us again. I love him so much and really am very sorry for putting my son through such a horrible time.

Looking back on the book I wrote I can see where I went wrong I was just a lost teenage girl getting involved in the wrong company and being easily lead. I always seemed to be in the wrong place at the wrong time if only I hadn't of been so strong minded in the first place then I would of listened to my mom and it would have been easy to bring me up. I know it wasn't easy for my mom she told me she would wait for the phone to ring and wait for the police to tell her I had been murdered. That's how dangerous I was. I would not be any one else but myself regardless what I went through

I know deep down in my heart that I'm a good hearted person and always will be and always have been. I was always involved in situations that hid the real Carrie. Now I think to myself how lucky I am and love the world no matter what war or disagreement's that are going on we are all one at the end of the day fighting and arguing   gets us nowhere .and everybody wants to be somewhere .

Don't make the same mistake's as I did don't find out the hard way, always trust your instincts and never allow anyone to overpower your mind. That is one thing that will always remain in tack no matter how many times your body gets battered. As long as you have your own mind they will never win ……

I'm just listening to some music I want to finish my book so I can move on to another project, what that will be I do not no. I got a confession to make to you all. In chapter one I said I was by the swimming pool in the manor ,,and I hope you did not think it was my manor , unfortunately it is not my house . It's one of my clients she only lives here at the weekends so I come to the house and use the pool and relax here. I wish it was my house, oh well a girl can dream cant she. I 'm happy with my house it's the best ever and would not swoop it for any house. It's perfect for me and my son and my dog. Isn't it funny how time seems to go so slow when you are going through a tough time and when you are having fun it just go's so fast. All those years of abuse felt like a life time to me and I never wish anyone to be in the same sort of problems I was. don't stand for it be strong move on as there is a brighter day and the proof is in the pudding , here I am on better days head strong enough to go back and write down what happened all through those years. It has been hard to do but I am glad I have done it now I feel like all the bad memories are now far at the back of my mind. I know I'm nobody special and I'm not famous but I have a storey that needs to be told, fifteen years of abusive relationships is what it finally took for me to see the light. All I can say is that maybe because I was beat up by a boyfriend at such a young age, I was just used to this sort of thing. People think I Must have been crazy to stay with it for so long and ask me why I did it. To be honest I just don't know and I'm ashamed that I let myself and my son go through this . I can't turn back the hands of time I can make sure I'm never going down that street again.

I would like to thank who ever reads this book and hope you enjoyed the true life story of ms Carrie Elwell. It wasn't an enjoyment living in fear day in and day out, but I hope I have painted a clear picture of the kind of person I really am and I hope you enjoyed the way I put the book together off the top of my head, I feel like I have got a lot off my chest .and no for a fact that no one or nothing can ever bring me down again. So any one who is feeling weak in any sort of situation they are in, just use your mind and you will get the result you want in the end…

Lightning Source UK Ltd.
Milton Keynes UK
07 May 2010

153854UK00001B/15/P